FLORIDA'S NEW DEAL
PARKS AND POST OFFICE
❧ M U R A L S ❦

KERI WATSON

THE
History
PRESS

Published by The History Press
Charleston, SC
www.historypress.com

First published 2024

Manufactured in the United States

ISBN 9781467156967

Library of Congress Control Number: 2023950629

Notice: The information in this book is true and complete to the best of our knowledge. It is offered without guarantee on the part of the author or The History Press. The author and The History Press disclaim all liability in connection with the use of this book.

Dedicated to Doris M. Prichard and Lucille G. Ortman

MILTON
DEFUNIAK SPRINGS
MARIANNA
PENSACOLA
BRISTOL
TALLAHASSEE
MADISON
JASPER
PERRY
FERNANDINA BEACH
JACKSONVILLE
HIGH SPRINGS
STARKE
KEYSTONE HEIGHTS
ST. AUGUSTINE
PALATKA
GAINESVILLE
ORLANDO
THONOTOSASSA
CLEARWATER
TAMPA
LAKE WALES
PALM BAY
ST. PETERSBURG
SARASOTA
SEBRING
ARCADIA
FORT PIERCE
WEST PALM BEACH
NAPLES
FORT LAUDERDALE
MIAMI
KEY WEST

CONTENTS

ACKNOWLEDGMENTS

As the granddaughter of a postmaster, I have long been captivated by the colorful murals that decorate the walls of post offices throughout the country, but the parks and post offices of Florida first captured my attention after I returned to my home state in 2014 for a faculty position in the School of Visual Arts and Design at the University of Central Florida. I am thankful to the University of Central Florida for a research grant that facilitated this project and to my husband, Cliff Watson, for traveling across the state with me and taking these photographs. My appreciation goes to the librarians and archivists at the National Archives and Records Administration, the Archives of American Art, and the State Archives of Florida and those researchers who contribute to online digital resources: the Living New Deal, Post Office Fans, and Postlandia. The primary sources you safekeep make a project such as this one possible. Thanks are due to Katherine Jentleson, Gisela Carbonell, Marcy Galbreath, and Amy Giroux, as well as audiences at the annual meetings of the College Art Association, Southeastern College Art Conference, and Florida College English Association, who have responded to parts of this research over the years. I am also indebted to my colleagues Akela Reason, Alexis Monroe, Gretchen Sinnett, Barbara Batson, Leah C. Tharpe, Anna O. Morley, Lee Ann Custer, Clarisse Fava-Piz, and Emily Ann Francisco— our conversations sponsored by the Association of Historians of American Art's reading groups have informed my thinking on this topic in countless ways. Thanks to the Florida Humanities Council for including me in its

Speakers Bureau and making this project a part of their "Florida Talks" series and to fellow Florida historian James C. Clark for your sage advice along the way. I appreciate the amazing design work of Matthew Dunn and Anna Burrous and Abigail Fleming's and Joe Gartrell's deft editorial hands; your enthusiasm for the project kept me going. Finally, thanks to my family: my son, Wes, and my husband, Cliff. I will forever treasure the time we spent together trekking across the state to visit parks and post offices. I am lucky to share life's adventures with you.

INTRODUCTION

Even before the stock market crashed on October 29, 1929, the Florida economy was depressed from two major hurricanes, a citrus export embargo, and the collapse of the real estate market. Florida desperately needed the relief promised by President Franklin Delano Roosevelt's New Deal and actively participated in and benefited from a number of federally sponsored initiatives during the Great Depression. These programs were aimed at what the president termed "Relief, Recovery, and Reform," and they affected every sector of society from banking and farming to art and architecture. *Florida's New Deal Parks and Post Office Murals* focuses on the state parks and post offices built in Florida between 1931 and 1946 under the auspices of the Civilian Conservation Corps, Public Works Administration, Civil Works Administration, Works Progress Administration, and Treasury Section of Painting and Sculpture. Looking at Florida's Depression-era parks and post offices in concert elucidates the ways in which the natural and built environments work together to constitute the cultural landscape and provides insight into the role of the federal government in Florida's construction as an exotic and tropical paradise.

"Florida, the southernmost State," remarked John J. Tigert, third president of the University of Florida, in his foreword to the *WPA Guide to Florida* (1939), "is frequently referred to as the last American frontier," and in many ways, Florida's history is bound up in the same issues of settler colonialism and environmental exploitation that marked westward expansion. Different publics and values exert their influence and authority over physical geographies, and Florida, as well as its place in the national imaginary, has changed over time. Its construction in parks and paintings has evolved, too, as shifting priorities and agendas influence what the land and its representations mean to the state's residents and visitors.

Art and the environment work hand in hand, as art has played a key role in both the destruction and preservation of the nation's scenic landscapes. During the nineteenth century, artists working in the Hudson River Valley created paintings of the region's lakes, rivers, and mountains to protect and preserve them, and the paintings of Yosemite and Yellowstone by Albert Bierstadt and Thomas Moran helped establish the National Park Service. At the same time, Frederick Law Olmsted molded the landscapes of Golden Gate Park in San Francisco and Central Park in New York into public gathering places that inculcated in the growing populace a love of nature. Florida's land and seascapes have provided similar aesthetic inspiration to artists whose work encouraged both development and conservation. From the work of William Bartram in the seventeenth century, John James Audubon in the eighteenth, and George Inness and Winslow Homer in the nineteenth to the post office muralists in the 1930s and 1940s, artists have represented Florida's natural landscape, shaping it to suit the tastes of contemporary viewing audiences. Studying artists' representations of the Florida landscape alongside plans developed by Florida's first park superintendents emphasizes the interconnectedness of nature and culture and asks us to examine how and where art and ecology intersect.

Traveling from the Panhandle to the Everglades, one encounters a variety of climates, flora, and fauna, and the state's rich and diverse landscapes of sand dunes, freshwater swamps, estuaries, bays, rivers, marshes, hardwood hammocks, dunes, mangroves, wetlands, and shrub lands are reflected in its post office murals and state parks. In fact, Florida is home to forty-five distinct terrestrial ecosystems. The Panhandle is marked by rolling hills, bluffs, and ravines, whereas the flatwoods of Central Florida offer small decreases in elevation that create depression marshes, dome swamps, and wet prairies, and South Florida is notable for its ponds and sloughs, sawgrass marshes, wetlands, hammock and cypress forests, and dry prairies. Florida's 1,200 miles of coastline, which include estuaries, seagrass beds, mangrove swamps, and coral reefs, along with inland freshwater lakes, rivers, streams, and springs, support thousands of aquatic communities, and as sea levels rise and fall, limestone deposits have created karst landscapes marked by sinkholes, caves, and artesian springs. Sand ridges in the central peninsula around present-day Sebring and Lake

Wales were once islands surrounded by the sea, which allowed unique species of plants and animals to evolve there. Finally, the state's climate varies from temperate in the north to tropical in the south, contributing to the establishment of distinct geologies and climates.

The modern environmental movement traces its origins to Progressive-era concerns over diminishing natural resources that necessitated their management, as well as to naturalists such as John Muir, who famously undertook his "walk to the Gulf" in 1867. With the establishment of the first state park in the Yosemite Valley (California) in 1870 and the first national park at Yellowstone (Wyoming and Montana) in 1872, however, the American interest in conservation yielded to state and national authority. As noted by art historian Naomi Slipp, by the 1870s, "national policy toward nature was driven by capitalism and focused on natural resource management, with the specific aim of maximizing commodity yield over time to increase profits." Fifty years later, anxieties over resources—both natural and human—would coincide with an expansion of government oversight under the New Deal as federal programs such as the Agricultural Administration, Soil Conservation Service, and Resettlement Administration were established to develop responsible land management strategies and prevent the types of environmental disasters that contributed to the Great Depression.

The guiding principle of Roosevelt's New Deal programs—whether led by the Treasury Section of Painting and Sculpture, the Public Works Administration, the Works Progress Administration, or the Civilian Conservation Corps—was to aid in the country's economic recovery by providing Americans with jobs, enrichment programs, and a social safety net. In 1936, as part of Roosevelt's New Deal, Congress passed the Federal Park, Parkway, and Recreational Area Study Act, which asked state planners to evaluate their conservation and recreation efforts and to create an inventory of properties that could be developed into parks. Funded by the Works Progress Administration, the Florida State Planning Board and the Florida Forestry and Parks Board completed their study, which found that "climate, natural recreation, and parks" were the state's main tourist attractions. Seeing an opportunity to use federal dollars to develop a system of state parks, Florida legislators designated Royal Palm State Park in Paradise Key (established as Florida's first state park in 1916) the site of the first Civilian Conservation Corps camp in the state. The Civilian Conservation Corps, which trained young men in construction and conservation techniques, was the first New Deal agency to begin operations in Florida. It employed more than forty-nine thousand men between 1933 and 1942, operating thirty-five camps across the state and establishing eight new parks: Florida Caverns State Park in Marianna, Torreya State Park in Rock Bluff, O'Leno State Park in High Springs, Mike Roess Gold Head Branch State Park in Keystone Heights, Fort Clinch State Park in Fernandina Beach, Highlands Hammock State Park in Sebring, Hillsborough River State Park in Thonotosassa, and Myakka River State Park in Sarasota. The Works Progress Administration assisted in constructing a ninth park, Ravine Gardens State Park in Palatka. Together these parks helped establish the Florida Park Service.

Florida's state parks (today there are 175 state parks encompassing nearly 800,000 acres in Florida) help preserve the unique natural ecosystems of the state. Unlike the rest of the nation, Florida's latitude makes it a temperate, subtropical, and tropical region with weather patterns determined less by fronts than by trade winds and westerlies. Driving from one end of the state to the other, you can see the climate change as the pines of the north are slowly and steadily replaced by palms. The parks of the state highlight these differences, as the state parks in North Florida feature caverns, springs, and river ravines; those of Central Florida highlight the pine flatwoods, wet prairies, temperate hardwood forests, and rock lands that mark its landscape; and the parks of South Florida preserve the nation's rare dry prairies, savannas, and subtropical wetlands.

In addition to conserving the state's unique and diverse ecosystems, the Florida Park Service preserves cultural sites that tell the history of the state. Florida's state parks are stewards of sacred Indigenous sites, they document the independence of the Native peoples who banded together to form the Seminole tribe, they tell the stories of those who self-emancipated by escaping slavery, and they outline the causes and stages of the American Civil War.

Art is a vital contributor to the creation and preservation of these stories, and although Roosevelt's New Deal programs were designed primarily to manage resources and provide work relief, in 1933, artist George Biddle encouraged his old college friend Roosevelt to extend his programs to artists, arguing that "our mural art with a little impetus can soon result, for the first time in our history, in a vital national expression." Believing that art would enrich the lives of all who encountered it, Roosevelt established the Public Works of Art Project (PWAP) in December 1933 to commission visual artists to create decorative embellishments for federal buildings. Over the course of its seven months, the PWAP funded 3,750 artists who produced 15,600 artworks at a cost of $1,312,000. Because of its success, the project was replaced with a permanent program, the Treasury Department's Section of

Painting and Sculpture, which was established six months later, on October 16, 1934. This program, more commonly called "the Section," sponsored more than 1,400 murals and close to 300 sculptures created by 850 different artists in 1,300 towns and cities between October 1934 and July 1943. With the Reorganization Act of 1939, the Public Buildings Administration took on the responsibilities of the Treasury's Public Buildings Branch, which constructed, maintained, and operated federal buildings such as post offices. The act also renamed the Treasury Section of Painting and Sculpture the Section of Fine Arts, but regardless of the name of the program, the expense of commissions was built into the construction costs of the post offices, with 1 percent of costs earmarked for decoration. Thus, the patronage of the Treasury Department enabled towns across the country to commission professional artists to create original works of art to adorn their post offices.

Unlike the Works Progress Administration programs, including the Federal Arts Project and the Treasury Relief Art Program, which provided commissions to artists based on economic need, the Section selected artists through regional contest or by invitation. Artists submitted drawings based on guidelines that specified subject matter and format, and juries of distinguished artists judged the applications. The best drawings were then sent to the national office in Washington, D.C., for final approval. Once the artist was selected, the design had to be accepted by both the national office and a local committee, often composed of the county's postmaster and other civic leaders. Sometimes artists were asked to modify their drawings submitted for one part of the country for use in other parts of the country, so a sketch originally intended for a post office in Maine might be modified to fit the needs of a post office in Florida.

Although strictly speaking a mural is a painting created directly on a wall, most of the murals created for post offices were in fact oil paintings on canvas that were then attached, often by glue, onto a wall, usually the horizontal space above the postmaster's door. Oil paintings had the advantage of being transferable and did not necessitate the artist being in residence for a long period of time, if at all. Although artists were encouraged to visit the site and meet the locals, scheduling conflicts and expenses sometimes prevented travel; therefore, artists did not always physically go to the post offices where their murals were to be installed. This could lead to resentment in cases where locals felt like their region was being stereotyped or misunderstood by a foreign artist or in cases where a local artist submitted a design but an artist from another part of the country was selected for the commission. Nearly all the artists involved in Florida mural commissions managed to make a trip to the town where their mural was to be installed, and four artists—Denman Fink, Joseph A. Myers, George Snow Hill, and Lucile Blanch—had lived in the state. Another artist, Constance Ortmayer, took a teaching position in Florida after completing her mural.

Despite the willingness of artists to travel to Florida and the selection of several local artists, there were still problems. In two cases, for commissions in Fort Pierce and Miami, local artists protested the selection of an artist from another state. Moreover, some Floridians in the 1930s felt alienated by the state's dependence on tourism and viewed any federally funded beautification project with suspicion. As Florida's population boomed—it increased 47 percent between 1930 and 1950, more than any other state in the country— some felt their livelihoods threatened by newcomers and resented the interference of outsiders from Washington, D.C. Despite these issues, most artists invited to create murals for post offices in Florida seemed to enjoy their work, and most municipalities were pleased with the resulting artwork.

The positive reception of Florida's murals may be related to the Section's insistence that morally uplifting themes prevail. Troubling, depressing, or overtly political subject matter, as well as nudity, was to be avoided, and mythological scenes, which were considered remote and illegible to many contemporary viewers, were discouraged. Instead, the Section preferred naturalistic images featuring scenes of regional or historical significance. Per the Section's instructions:

Specific subjects include the postal service and its history; methods of communication and transportation; specific events or individuals in national or local history; American Indians; the exploration and settlement of America or the locality; agriculture, conservation, and rural life; local products, industry, and commerce; and allegorical themes such as law, justice, progress, and the inter-relationship of industry and agriculture.

The Section's guidelines are reflected in Florida's post office murals, which depict events such as European encounters with Indigenous peoples; include representations of popular landmarks such as the Jupiter Lighthouse and the Bok Tower; feature historical figures including Ponce de León, Hernando de Soto, Andrew Jackson, and Chief Osceola; and offer scenes of industry and agriculture, such as growing citrus or cutting timber.

Between 1938 and 1946, from Milton to Miami, artists were hired by the Treasury Section of Painting and Sculpture (renamed the Section of Fine Arts in 1939) to paint murals and carve relief sculptures to decorate Florida's newly built post offices. Today, these examples of public art offer glimpses of Florida's past and illustrate the importance of federal art patronage during the Great Depression. Created amid a flurry of unprecedented federal and local government support for artists, post office murals made art a part of everyday life, and in many parts of the country, including Florida, they gave people their first encounter with original works of art. Sixteen post offices were built in Florida during the Great Depression, and each featured art commissioned by the federal government.

Although the Civil Works Administration and Works Progress Administration built the post offices, it was the Section that decorated them, and whereas the Section commissioned artwork for courthouses and other federal buildings as well as post offices, it is the post office murals for which it is best remembered. Post offices were the perfect place to reach people, and under the leadership of Director Edward Bruce and Assistant Director Edward Rowan, the Section provided work and recognition to artists while bringing art into the everyday lives of average Americans, free of charge. The work was derided by some: a 1977 article for the *New York Times* claimed, "The term 'post office mural' became for many critics a term of abuse, and artists themselves—especially if they had won new reputations as members of the avant-garde—sometimes suppressed their own former works." Today, some eighty years after they were painted, most murals are admired by locals and tourists alike and studied as important documents of U.S. history.

Still, some post office murals have come under fire in recent years. In the fall of 2020, the United States Postal Service ordered the staff at sixteen post offices in twelve states, including Florida, to cover their murals. They issued the following statement to explain their decision:

> *In past decades, artwork has been placed in Post Office lobbies for permanent public display. Traditionally, Post Office lobbies were community gathering spots, frequently visited by community members from all walks of life, making those locations particularly accessible display sites.*
>
> *The Postal Service respects and embraces the uniqueness and diversity of every individual. And we encourage contributions of people from different backgrounds, experiences, and perspectives, including those of our employees and members of the communities we serve.*
>
> *While it is the policy of the Postal Service to preserve and protect the historic artwork in its collection for future generations, we are mindful that certain murals generate strong feelings for some of our employees and customers.*

With that in mind, discussions are being held on how to properly handle and safeguard the future of those pieces. We are evaluating each of the pieces and we will work to ensure that appropriate action is taken on select murals, if deemed necessary.

The murals under evaluation, which include George Snow Hill's painting in the post office in Madison, Florida, have been covered with dark-colored plastic sheets, making them inaccessible to viewers. Although the U.S. Postal Service has not said why some of its murals are being covered, all but three of the paintings under scrutiny are in the South and fifteen of them depict antebellum scenes. Thirteen represent enslaved laborers working in either the cotton (eight), tobacco (two), or sugarcane (one) industries. Another includes a depiction of two shirtless Black laborers plowing a field (Newton, Mississippi). At least one of the murals (*Golden Triangle of Trade*, Medford, Massachusetts) has been covered before, and others, such as the mural for the post office in Louisburg, North Carolina, which represents a tobacco auction, have inspired protest. Three other post offices with "American Indian themed mural[s]" have also received complaints from customers, but they have not been covered. Instead, explanatory labels written by Daniel Delahaye, the current U.S. federal preservation officer, have been posted adjacent to the murals.

Public art has never been immune to controversy, as definitions of who comprises the public and what constitutes art are complex and contentious questions. Nelson Rockefeller ordered the destruction of Diego Rivera's mural *Man at the Crossroads* shortly after it was completed in 1933, and Richard Serra's sculpture *Tilted Arc* (1981) was removed from Manhattan's Foley Plaza in 1989, but the U.S. Postal Service has historically prevented the censor of the murals under its care (as art funded with federal dollars, they are the property of the people). As recently as July 2020, the U.S. Postal Service, following the guidelines set forth by the Fine Arts Policies and Procedures of the General Services Administration, asserted, "Our policy has always been not to cover or remove these artworks based on one person or group's artistic interpretation, but to preserve the works in our custody for future generations." Thus, the move just a month later in August 2020 to cover sixteen murals and consider their removal marks a significant change in public policy.

This shift is likely the result of increased pressure from citizens and the recognition that public institutions that present art have a responsibility to mitigate the traumatizing effects of the representations they display. Shardae

Vines collected three hundred signatures on her petition to remove Richard Kenah's mural of a tobacco auction from the post office in Louisburg, North Carolina. She justified its removal, saying, "This painting depicts white farmers buying and selling tobacco in an auction and shows African American men working without shirts and shoes. This is just one more unnecessary reminder of the inhumane conditions our African American ancestors were subjected to in an effort to survive economically all while building the wealth of this nation." Or, as art historian Anna Arabindan-Kesson argues about plantation scenes in general, "Plantation representations functioned as an emblem of a planter's status.…It is impossible to look and not see plantations and back-breaking labor, not see centuries of racial exploitation and oppression, not see this history repeated in the carceral system, in police brutality, in the economic and legislative marginalization of African Americans."

The latest controversy over post office murals finds precedents in the debates over Confederate monuments and other public art. Some 160 monuments and memorials to the Confederate States of America have been removed from public spaces since 2015, and in Bloomington, Indiana, students have called for the removal of Thomas Hart Benton's mural made for the 1933 Century of Progress Exhibition in Chicago because it includes representations of the Ku Klux Klan. In San Francisco, California, students and community members have called for the removal of Victor Arnautoff's 1936 mural for George Washington High School because it depicts enslaved African Americans and shows Washington stepping over the body of a dead Native American, and in Lexington, Kentucky, students have denounced Ann Rice O'Hanlon's 1934 mural for the university "as a racist sanitizing of history and a painful reminder of slavery." Wendell Berry sued the university over its removal of the painting in a suit supported by Karyn Olivier, a Black artist who created a mural in 2018 that hangs adjacent to O'Hanlon's piece. Olivier argues that the removal of O'Hanlon's mural jeopardizes her own work, which "is dependent on that history." Whereas some of these debates, like those surrounding the removal of Confederate monuments, have received national attention, the recent covering of post office murals has gone largely unnoticed.

For many, these monuments and murals perpetuate myths of both the Lost Cause and the Old South, ideologies prevalent in the 1930s that claimed the Civil War was fought over states' rights rather than slavery. In the midst of the Great Depression, as farmers were pushed off their land and the boll weevil ravaged cotton crops, some found solace in looking back nostalgically on a period of agricultural abundance. The first Natchez Pilgrimage was organized by the Natchez Garden Club in 1932, and the national press often focused on the South's "antebellum pride" in magazine articles that framed the South as an agricultural paradise. As southern tourism increased, the South was often framed in pastoral terms, and although recent interpretive efforts acknowledge the horrors of slavery and attend to the lives of those women and men held in bondage, during the 1930s idealized images of plantation homes and enslaved laborers à la *Gone with the Wind*, which made their way into post office murals, were common. "Bowered in magnolia trees and dogwood and fiery azaleas, the young actors in that poignant drama of the Old South, the Confederate Ball, dance," the February 1938 issue of *Better Homes and Gardens* opined, in an article aptly titled "The Old South Lives Again."

For years, post office murals depicting, and in many cases glorifying, the "Old South" seemed to have exemplified what Dell Upton termed a "dual heritage" that allowed southerners, White and Black, to acknowledge the Black past without relinquishing White mythologies, but since the Charleston church shooting in 2015 and the murder of George Floyd in 2020, calls to remove symbols of the Confederacy, the "Old South," and enslavement from public spaces have increased. These debates ignite important conversations about the connection between the Middle Passage, the establishment of the plantation economy, and the ecological crises that have dramatically affected the natural environment and our place within it. The relationship between parks and post offices then is an important one, as it not only illustrates art's role in the recreation of the natural world but also reveals deeply held beliefs and biases about the landscape and lays bare the unequal effects of climate change on different populations and geographies. Biddle promised Roosevelt that artists working for the federal government "would be contributing to and expressing in living monuments the social ideals that you are struggling to achieve," but social ideals are not static. Attending to the history of Florida's state parks, as well as the art of the southern landscape and calls for its effacement, reveals the ways art and ecology construct, reflect, reinforce, and subvert systems of power.

Although George Snow Hill's mural for the Madison Post Office, which depicts Black workers in the town's cotton gin, is the only mural in Florida that is currently covered, there are other accessibility issues related to viewing Florida's post office murals. The painting for the Starke Post Office was destroyed during a lobby renovation in the 1980s, and one expects that the only reason Hill's mural for the post office in Milton, which depicts Black and White men playing dice on a riverboat, is not covered is because it is now in the collection of the Santa Rosa Historical Society. (Ironically, it was covered by White civic leaders in the 1950s and 1960s, who found its image of an integrated workforce unsettling.) As the nation's post office murals, many of which include problematic representations of the past and perpetuate negative stereotypes of Indigenous peoples and Black Americans, come under increased public and scholarly scrutiny, it becomes even more urgent to document these paintings. New Deal–era murals chronicle an important moment in history. They represent the beliefs and values, however troubling, of their artists and patrons, and many of them include depictions of the landscape that provide insights into the relationship between the natural and built environments at a crucial moment in Florida's and the nation's development.

The diversity of the state's ecology and the conflicts and compromises of its history are reflected in its state parks, its post office murals, and in the architecture of the post offices themselves. Offering an alternative view of Florida, this work presents readers with photographs of Florida's parks and post offices; the post office's murals and the buildings they decorate; insights into their relationship to their communities, past and present; and information about the people who made them. Divided into three parts that correspond to the main geographical regions of the state: North, Central, and South, *Florida's New Deal Parks and Post Office Murals* acts as both a tourist's guide to Florida's parks and post offices and a primary source for those interested in art, the environment, and the New Deal. It discusses Florida's post office murals, the municipalities where they are found, and the artists who made them, as well as the history of Florida's original state parks built by the Civilian Conservation Corps, Civil Works Administration, and Works Progress Administration. Suggested routes and a map are included. I hope you enjoy this journey through Florida as much as I did and that it will prompt you to consider the interdependence of art and nature.

I

NORTH FLORIDA

N orth Florida, as defined by the state's economic development agency and the Florida Department of Transportation, stretches from Perdido Key in Escambia County in the west to Fernandina Beach in Nassau County in the east and down through the Big Bend to Levy and Flagler Counties in the south. The region's largest cities are Pensacola, Tallahassee, Jacksonville, and Gainesville.

The Civil Works Administration and Works Progress Administration built seven post offices in North Florida between 1938 and 1942, and each was decorated with murals commissioned by the Treasury Section of Painting and Sculpture. Thirteen Depression-era murals, reflective of the region's history and industry, were hung in post offices in Milton, DeFuniak Springs, Tallahassee, Perry, Madison, and Starke, and two true fresco murals were painted on the walls of the post office in Jasper. North Florida's post office murals were made by well-respected and award-winning artists, two of whom—Thomas Laughlin and Elizabeth Terrell—had their post office mural designs featured in the December 1939 issue of *Life* magazine as part of the "48 States Competition." Colorful murals were created by George Snow Hill in Milton, Madison, and Perry; Thomas Laughlin in DeFuniak Springs; and Pietro Lazzari in Jasper, but the most famous murals in North Florida are the eight paintings collectively titled *History of Florida* and completed in 1939 by Hungarian-born American artist Eduard "Buk" Ulreich for the post office and courthouse in Tallahassee. Unfortunately,

Elizabeth Terrell's mural for the post office in Starke was destroyed during a lobby renovation in the 1980s, but a copy of the black-and-white sketch she submitted to the Section is extant and offers documentation of the commission.

North Florida boasts six state parks established by three other New Deal programs: the Works Progress Administration, the Civil Works Administration, and the Civilian Conservation Corps. The Civil Works Administration was a job creation program that provided jobs for millions of unemployed workers during the winter of 1933–34. The Works Progress Administration, established by executive order on May 6, 1935, put millions of jobseekers to work building public works such as schools, courthouses, hospitals, bridges, and roads. The Civilian Conservation Corps was established on March 31, 1933, to address land management and unemployment. By 1930, much of the nation's forests had been depleted, leading to the erosion of as much as six billion tons of soil annually. At the same time, some two million people, a quarter of the nation's labor force, were out of work. The Civilian Conservation Corps hired unemployed laborers to work on projects supervised by the U.S. Forest Service. Between 1933 and 1942, the Civilian Conservation Corps, nicknamed Roosevelt's "Tree Army," planted two billion trees, slowed soil erosion on forty million acres of farmland, and built eight hundred new state parks across the nation.

The first New Deal agency to begin operations in Florida, the Civilian Conservation Corps employed more than forty-nine thousand Floridians between 1933 and 1942. In 1930, Florida's unemployment rate hovered around 25 percent, and by 1935, Florida ranked second in the nation in per capita enrollment of citizens in the Civilian Conservation Corps. Florida's landscape had changed dramatically since 1900 with waterways drained and diverted and agriculture replacing natural ecosystems, but the Corps rehabilitated marshes and swamplands; developed new roads; put in place controlled burn plans to revitalize forests; and created new waterways, such as canals and man-made lakes, to improve drainage. Enrollees planted thirteen million trees in Florida, operated thirty-five camps throughout the state, and helped develop the Florida Park Service (FPS) by establishing Florida's first state parks. Between 1933 and 1942, the Civilian Conservation Corps assisted the state in constructing 5 parks in North Florida: Florida Caverns State Park in Marianna, Torreya State Park in Rock Bluff, O'Leno State Park in High Springs, Mike Roess Gold Head Branch State Park in Keystone Heights, and Fort Clinch State Park in Fernandina Beach. The Works Progress Administration (WPA) helped build a sixth park, Ravine Gardens State Park in Palatka. Most of these parks would be closed to the public or transitioned to military usage by 1943 but were reopened to the public after the end of the Second World War. Today the Florida Parks Service (FPS) operates 175 parks across the state, and the system has been recognized for its excellence.

Six of the ten original state parks in Florida are in North Florida, and the buildings, structures, and cultural landscapes of these parks exemplify "the rustic style" of park architecture promoted by Herbert Maier and Thomas Chalmers Vint of the National Park Service. Their approach to park development was codified in two pattern books compiled in the 1930s: the U.S. Forest Service's *Recreation Plans Handbook* (1936) and Albert Good's *Park and Recreation Structures* (1938). These books became the standard pattern books for park development during the New Deal and led to the construction of similar buildings and structures across the nation. At the same time, the master planning of each park responded to the features and materials of its location, which encouraged the development of diverse landscapes. In North Florida, where locally sourced building materials included limestone, cypress, and pine, a unique cultural landscape emerged as men working on the Civilian Conservation Corps built distinctly faced picnic facilities, cabins, administrative buildings, and fences in order to make the parks available, accessible, and appealing to the general public. The Civilian Conservation Corps also restored historic buildings, worked on fire prevention and management—including creating firebreaks and conducting controlled burns to reduce the risk of wildfires—and engaged in conservation education and public outreach programs that helped raise awareness about the importance of preserving natural resources.

Part I takes readers on a tour of North Florida's post offices and parks. Beginning in the northwestern corner of the state and traversing the Panhandle, it includes stops in Milton, DeFuniak Springs, Marianna, Rock Bluff, Tallahassee, Perry, Madison, Jasper, High Springs, Starke, Keystone Heights, Palatka, and Fernandina Beach. The suggested route makes for a full itinerary on a weeklong vacation with overnight stays at six state parks. Alternatively, each destination makes for a nice day trip.

GEORGE SNOW HILL (1898–1969)

Loading Pulpwood, 1941

MILTON POST OFFICE
6866 CAROLINE STREET
MILTON, FL 32570

Nestled in the northwest corner of Florida just north of Pensacola you'll find Milton, one of the oldest cities in the state. Originally known as "Scratch Ankle" because of the briars that grew wild in the area, Milton was established in the 1830s between the Blackwater Bay and River as a mill town. Settler John Hunt developed a brickyard and a sawmill there and encouraged the Alabama, Florida, and Georgia Railroad to build a depot for the transport of lumber. Beginning in the early nineteenth century, settlers felled the longleaf pines that once covered between sixty and ninety million acres of the Southeastern Coastal Plain and sold the lumber for shipbuilding and railroads. By 1850, the lumber industry was well established in North Florida, with most of the steam-powered mills employing between six and eight laborers and producing about 300,000 to 450,000 board feet of lumber per year (or about 1,300 board feet per day). By 1909, more than 16 billion board feet of lumber were produced annually in North Florida from the longleaf pines that were once so abundant that they seemed like an inexhaustible resource. By the 1920s, most of them were gone, and today, they are endangered. Restoration has become a priority in recent years, because longleaf pines are a keystone species that provide habitat for more than thirty endangered species. Although thousands of acres of slash pine are now being converted back to longleaf pine, less than 5 percent of the original acreage remains.

The cornerstone for the Milton Post Office was laid in 1940 under the direction of federal works administrator John M. Carmody and supervising architect Louis A. Simon (fig. 1.1). Simon spent most of his career in the Office of the Supervising Architect of the U.S. Treasury and was responsible for the introduction of a standard building plan that could be quickly constructed and then dressed in an architectural style appropriate to the region, whether Colonial Revival, Spanish Colonial Revival, Art Deco, or other options. Located at 6821 Caroline Street, the Milton Post Office is a classic example of the standard plan adorned with elements of the Colonial Revival style (fig. 1.2). It includes red brick accented with

1.1 Cornerstone of the Milton Post Office, Milton, Florida, laid in 1940 at 6821 Caroline Street under the direction of federal works administrator John M. Carmody. *Photograph by Cliff Watson, courtesy of the author.*

1.2 Exterior of the Milton Post Office, Milton, Florida. This Colonial Revival–style post office was commissioned by the Works Progress Administration and built in 1940. *Photograph by Cliff Watson, courtesy of the author.*

engaged concrete pilasters, a large-paned transom window above the double-doored entrance, a shingled hip roof, and a cupola crowned with a weathervane. Nearly identical post offices can be found across the country from Lancaster, New York, to Adel, Georgia.

The mural that once decorated the lobby of the Milton Post Office on Caroline Street depicts the lumber industry on which the town was built. Although timber production was in decline by 1940, artist George Snow Hill opted for a scene of Black and White laborers on a pine-log raft ferrying logs downriver to a paper mill (Plate 1). In the foreground, men play dice and smoke cigarettes. The setting is marked as contemporary by the men's clothing and the late model car included on the stone arch bridge in the background. A church's bell tower, perhaps a symbol of the prosperity ensured by hard work and perseverance, is visible in the distance. The painting is representational, and Hill's style follows that of the then popular American Scene Movement, which was privileged by the Section. Hill's elongated figures and frenetic composition are especially reminiscent of the work of Thomas Hart Benton, as is his use of bold color. Like Benton, Hill developed a style that included what some called "cartoonish caricatures." As a result, Hill was later accused of creating racist portrayals of African Americans, and in 1966 a mural he painted for the city hall in St. Petersburg was ripped off the wall by burglars. As reported by the *St. Petersburg Times*, "It was a milestone in peaceful St. Petersburg's race relations this tearing down of a mural." Hill's reliance on physiognomic stereotypes in his depictions of African Americans as well as the distribution of the figures is concerning. Although Black and White men worked side by side as laborers in the logging industry of North Florida, Hill's inclusion of six Black workers and one White overseer in *Loading Pulpwood* reinforces racial segregation and Jim Crow values. Ironically, the mural was covered by a sheet during the 1950s and 1960s because some people found its inclusion of White and Black figures supportive of integration.

Born in Munising, Michigan, in 1898, Hill studied naval engineering and architecture at Lehigh University before transferring to Syracuse University to focus on art. He continued his pursuit of painting and sculpture abroad in Paris at the Académie Colarossi and the Académie de la Grande Chaumière but returned to the United States in 1929. He lived in New York City until 1932, when he moved to St. Petersburg, Florida, where he was met with immediate local success and helped establish an artist colony and school. The Art Club of St. Petersburg, today the St. Petersburg Museum of Fine Arts, celebrated his arrival with an exhibition

1.3 Exterior of the Imogene Theatre, Milton, Florida. Built after the great fire of 1909 destroyed the Milton commercial district, the theater closed in 1946. It was acquired by the Santa Rosa Historical Society in 1985 and reopened as a museum in 1987. *Photograph by Cliff Watson, courtesy of the author.*

in February 1933, and in addition to the post office murals he completed for the Treasury Section, he also painted Federal Art Project murals for the Pinellas County Courthouse in Clearwater, the Coast Guard Station in St. Petersburg, and the Janus Administration Building in Tampa. His murals decorated the Florida buildings at the 1933 Century of Progress Exhibition in Chicago and the 1939 New York World's Fair.

Hill's mural for the Milton Post Office was dedicated on November 11, 1940, and must have offered contemporary viewers a reminder of more prosperous times when virgin timber awaiting harvest covered the landscape. When a new post office was built in 1984, the mural was moved to the Santa Rosa Historical Society Museum. Following the Great Fire of 2009, which destroyed much of downtown Milton, the mural was temporarily stored back at the original Milton Post Office on Caroline Street (then an antique store) before it was rehung at the Imogene Theatre (fig. 1.3). It can be viewed by appointment.

THOMAS EARLE LAUGHLIN (1887–1964)

Scene of Town, 1942

DEFUNIAK SPRINGS POST OFFICE
100 SOUTH EIGHTEENTH STREET
DEFUNIAK SPRINGS, FL 32435

Located just sixty miles east of Milton, the idyllic hamlet of DeFuniak Springs features a French Colonial–style post office constructed with Treasury Department funds under the supervision of architect Louis A. Simon in 1938. The New Deal building (fig. 1.4), which is similar to the post office in Starke constructed three years later, is located at the northwest corner of Highway 90 and Seventh Street. It is now a privately owned business, but the mural can be viewed in the new post office on South Eighteenth Street that was built in 1989.

DeFuniak Springs was founded in 1881 by officers of the Pensacola and Atlantic Railroad as a destination resort town. It was named after Colonel Frederick DeFuniak, an Italian immigrant and executive of the Louisville-Nashville Railroad, who allegedly won the town's naming rights in a card game. Members of the Chautauqua Assembly, an educational group founded in 1874 in southwestern New York, helped develop the town along the banks of the spring-fed Lake DeFuniak (fig. 1.5). It quickly became a favorite winter retreat for Chautauqua members.

Thomas Laughlin, who studied at the Rhode Island School of Design and worked as a draftsman and sketch artist for a landscape architect in Philadelphia, was invited to submit a design for the DeFuniak Springs Post Office, but his prize-winning gouache of the mural (fig. 1.6), which was printed in *Life* magazine in December 1939, bears little resemblance to the mural installed in the post office in 1942 (Plate 2). Illustrating the gulf between North Florida's actual ecology and its perception in the national imaginary, *Life* described Laughlin's design as, "show[ing] the boats and fishermen that are a common sight in Florida." One of forty-eight winners selected out of 1,475 submissions, the sketch received national attention, but local jurors, including Postmaster Marie M. Stinson and members of the Women's Club, felt an ocean scene was not appropriate for DeFuniak Springs, a location notable for its spring-fed lake and rolling hills. Situated on the Dougherty Plain, DeFuniak Springs is thirty-plus miles from the Gulf of Mexico and epitomizes a typical karst topography marked by lime

Top: 1.4 Old DeFuniak Springs Post Office, DeFuniak Springs, Florida. Built with Treasury Section funds in 1938. Now privately owned. *Photograph by Cliff Watson, courtesy of the author.*

Bottom: 1.5 Lake DeFuniak and Chipley Park. This 260-acre park surrounds the perfectly round 40-acre naturally spring-fed Lake DeFuniak. This park and lake are the centerpiece of the historical district of DeFuniak Springs. *Photograph by Cliff Watson, courtesy of the author.*

sink ponds, marshes, and sinkholes. Feeling that Laughlin, who was born in Maine, would not be able to capture the beauty of the North Florida landscape, Hollis Holbrook of the University of Florida even sent an appeal to Washington asking them to choose a different artist. (Holbrook was also a Section artist, and his 1941 mural *Sugar Cane Mill*, created for the post office in Jeanerette, Louisiana, is one of the sixteen murals recently covered by the United States Postal Service.)

1.6 Thomas Laughlin sketch, *Life* magazine, December 1939. Laughlin significantly changed his design at the direction of the postmaster. *Courtesy of* Life *magazine.*

The Section responded to Holbrook's critique by asking Laughlin to submit a new design. Laughlin agreed, as his award-winning gouache had been a revision of a design that he had originally submitted for a post office in Maine. He realized that he would need to visit DeFuniak Springs to get a feel for the town. While there in October 1941, he sketched the lake and worked up a composition featuring the town's historical downtown area. Laughlin wrote to Assistant Director Rowan, explaining the lack of industry in his new sketch: "The Turpentine and lumber business were finished years ago so that with the exception of historical themes of Florida, or a decorative design of the town itself, my subject matter should be as good as any other." He submitted a revised design to the national office, and on November 17, 1941, it was approved. Laughlin was given nine months to complete the mural, for which he was paid $740. The finished painting, which offers a folksy, multiple-perspectival view of Lake DeFuniak and its historic buildings, is reminiscent of a picture postcard and appealed to contemporary viewers, who appreciated its blend of the natural and built environment.

When the new post office was built in 1989, the mural was moved, and a portion of it (including the bottom of the lake) was cut out so that it would fit in the space above the postmaster's door. Even with a portion of the mural removed, many of DeFuniak Springs's important landmarks are still visible. At the top of the painting is the Chautauqua Hall of Brotherhood (fig. 1.7); to its right is St. Agatha's Episcopal Church (fig. 1.8). The Walton-DeFuniak Library (fig. 1.9), the oldest continually operating library in Florida (it opened in 1887), can be found in the lower right corner of the painting. Also visible are the L&N Train Depot and the Chautauqua Vineyard. The stately Sunbright Manor with its octagonal tower, two round windows, wraparound porches, thirty-three columns, and 1,600 spindles is visible in the upper left.

1.7 Exterior of the Chautauqua Brotherhood. Built in 1909, the meeting hall of the Chautauqua Brotherhood hosted lectures, classes, and concerts in its four-thousand-seat auditorium. *Photograph by Cliff Watson, courtesy of the author.*

1.8 Exterior of the St. Agatha Episcopal Church. Construction of the Carpenter Gothic–style church began in 1895 under the direction of the Right Reverend Edwin G. Weed. It is part of the Episcopal Diocese of the Central Gulf Coast and the DeFuniak Springs Historic District. *Photograph by Cliff Watson, courtesy of the author.*

1.9 Historic DeFuniak Springs Library. Opened in 1887, it is the oldest continuously run library in Florida. It is part of the DeFuniak Springs Historic District. *Photograph by Cliff Watson, courtesy of the author.*

1.10 "Florida Education Association" historical marker, Florida Division of Historical Resources, Florida Department of State. The first meeting of the Florida Education Association, today a statewide federation of teachers whose 145,000 members make it the largest union in the state, had its first meeting here in 1886. *Photograph by Cliff Watson, courtesy of the author.*

Recently named one of the best small towns in Florida, DeFuniak Springs was also host to an important meeting that changed the course of public education in Florida. In 1886, teachers from around the state met in DeFuniak Springs and formed the Florida Education Association, the state's teachers' union (fig. 1.10). Today, the FEA is the largest union in Florida, with more than 145,000 members. Certainly a town full of history and nineteenth-century charm, DeFuniak Springs hosts an impressive display of lights, "Christmas Reflections," during the holidays.

Florida Caverns State Park

3345 Caverns Road
Marianna, FL 32446

Located about halfway between DeFuniak Springs and Tallahassee, Florida Caverns State Park opened in 1942 under the direction of Clarence Simpson, an eleven-year veteran of the Florida Geological Survey. The 1,500-acre park, which was built with the help of the Civilian Conservation Corps, features caverns, a natural spring swimming area, and hiking trails.

In the early twentieth century, the Florida Geological Survey conducted explorations in the area and documented the caves, but it wasn't until the 1930s that the site's potential for tourism and recreational use was recognized. Harry Baker, a civic leader who suggested that Florida use federal dollars to develop a state park system, called Marianna the "gateway to Florida for tourist travel," and noted that more than 500,000 of the 1,395,650 people who visited Florida in 1935 drove through Marianna. He saw the marketing of Florida's unique natural features—such as its caverns and springs—key to increasing its tourism dollars. As he said, "[People] are willing to spend their money in order to see things for which Florida is famous."

In this case, Marianna would become known for its limestone caverns (Plate 3), which formed over millions of years through the dissolution of limestone rock by acidic groundwater. The caverns include a network of underground chambers, passages, stalactites, stalagmites, and other unique rock formations. There is also evidence that Native Americans knew about the caves long before the arrival of European settlers and used them for shelter and ceremonial purposes.

1.11 "Park visitors enjoying the Blue Hole Spring swimming area at Florida Caverns State Park in Marianna," June 17, 1968. *Tallahassee Democrat* Collection, Florida Memory Project. *Courtesy of the State Archives of Florida.*

Part of a concerted effort to bring more tourists to North Florida, Florida Caverns State Park gave motorists a reason to stop on their way to more popular destinations in Central and South Florida. Young men working for the Civilian Conservation Corps added lights and enlarged the passageways by hand so visitors could stand upright during tours, and the marks left by their chisels are still visible today. Guided tours lead visitors through more than a dozen rooms that feature stalactites, rimstone pools, soda straws, calcite, and helictites. The Civilian Conservation Corps also built the park's visitor center and a nearby nine-hole golf course. By making the caverns into a state park, the Civilian Conservation Corps helped preserve the caves for future travelers, and over the years, the park has undergone various improvements and developments to enhance the visitor experience while preserving the natural environment. Today, this ancient underground formation provides a unique recreational opportunity for the public.

Also of interest at Florida Caverns State Park is Blue Hole Spring (Plate 4). One of more than one thousand springs in the state, Blue Hole Spring (fig. 1.11) is fed by a natural vent thirty-eight and a half feet below the surface of the earth that keeps the water seventy-two degrees Fahrenheit year-round. As the nearby Chipola River rises and falls throughout the year, the water feeding the spring passes through layers of limestone, causing the clarity and color of the water to change. The spring also is an important historical landmark. Spanish missionaries and soldiers crossed the nearby Natural Bridge of the Chipola River and traveled by Blue Hole in June 1674 on their way to establish Mission San Carlos and Mission San Nicolas just west of the park. Andrew Jackson passed through in 1818 during the First Seminole War and his cartographer made note of the spring. The spring was transformed into a swimming destination by workers with the Civilian Conservation Corps who added the dock and beach.

This type of transformation was not uncommon in the 1930s, as the Civilian Conservation Corps and the representatives of the state balanced the demands of conservation and recreation. The Florida Park Service actively promoted its park with printed pamphlets such as the sixteen-page glossy brochure *Florida State Parks Invite You*, which highlighted interesting sites such as Marianna's caverns and spring. At Florida Caverns State Park, the Civilian Conservation Corps blazed the Bluff and Beech Magnolia Trails, which feature rare Appalachian plant species and rock outcroppings used by Native Americans, as well as the Sinkhole Trail, which traverses through floodplains, sinkholes, caves, and streams. These trails can still be hiked today, or you can stay at one of the park's thirty-eight campsites.

TORREYA STATE PARK

2576 NORTHWEST TORREYA PARK ROAD
ROCK BLUFF, FL 32321

After visiting the caverns in Marianna, you can stop by Torreya State Park in Rock Bluff, a popular park for birding, camping, hiking, and picnicking. One of Florida's first state parks, Torreya was established in 1935 as part of the government's efforts to create jobs and preserve natural areas.

The park was named after the rare Florida torreya tree (*Torreya taxifolia*), one of the oldest tree species in North America and one that grows only on the bluffs above the Apalachicola River. Discovered in the 1830s by Hardy Bryan Croom and named for American botanist John Torrey, the torreya tree is notable for its distinctive appearance: short, flat needles and small, bristly cones (fig. 1.12). Considered a living fossil, the torreya is one of the oldest surviving tree species, with a lineage dating back 100 million years. Nineteenth-century settlers called it the "stinking cedar" because of its strong odor, and it was used for a variety of purposes, including fence posts, shingles, riverboat fuel, and Christmas trees. Scientists report that the torreya once lived across North America and estimate that there were 600,000 torreya trees living in the Apalachicola River Valley during the early 1800s. Although once widespread across the southeastern United States, the torreya has suffered from habitat loss and diseases that have diminished its range and population. The park's establishment aimed to protect this unique tree species and its surrounding natural environment, but unfortunately, Hurricane Michael (2018) knocked out 88 percent of the park's trees, and today it is considered a critically endangered species—only 200 remain.

1.12 Example of a torreya tree from Torreya State Park, Rock Bluff, Florida, 1938. Florida Park Service Collection, Florida Memory Project. *Courtesy of the State Archives of Florida.*

In addition to the presence of the torreya tree, the park is notable for its elevated plateaus (150 feet above sea level), steep bluffs that provide exceptionally scenic views, and stone bridges constructed by the Civilian Conservation Corps (Plate 5). To increase tourism, early brochures compared the park to more mountainous sites in Virginia, North Carolina, and Tennessee and claimed that there was "evidence of a forgotten Indian village" on the park grounds. Visitors were encouraged to gather Native American artifacts while visiting and to take a guided tour of the historic Gregory House (Plate 6), an antebellum mansion built in 1849 by Calhoun County planter and enslaver Jason Gregory. Confederate army and navy officers occasionally visited the home, and some of those injured when the CSS *Chattahoochee* exploded were brought there for care during the Civil War. The home was in disrepair by the time the park was established, but the Civilian Conservation Corps dismantled it, relocated it across the Apalachicola River to the park's property and reconstructed it on the bluff. At one point, the Corps planned to turn the Gregory House into a bed-and-breakfast, although these plans never materialized.

Since its opening, Torreya State Park has been a popular destination for outdoor enthusiasts, hikers, and nature lovers, who have recorded more than one hundred different species of birds in the park. It has twenty-nine campsites, two yurts, and a cabin that sleeps six.

Eduard "Buk" Ulreich (1884–1966)
History of Florida, 1939

Tallahassee Bankruptcy Courthouse
110 East Park Avenue #100
Tallahassee, FL 32301

From Torreya State Park, it's just fifty miles to Tallahassee. Here you'll find the Treasury Section–commissioned murals for the Tallahassee Post Office in the lobby of the bankruptcy courthouse. Postal services moved to a new building in the early 1970s, but the murals stayed behind.

Tallahassee, which means "old fields" in Muskogean, has enjoyed habitation since 1200 CE, when Native Americans of the Mississippian Culture built mounds near Lake Jackson. Later members of the Apalachee and then Seminole Nations moved into the area, and Spanish explorer Hernando de Soto wintered there in 1538–39. During the seventeenth century, several Spanish missions were established in the territory, and during the First Seminole War, General Andrew Jackson fought two separate battles in and around Tallahassee. Tallahassee became the capital of the Florida Territory in 1824, when it was chosen because it was roughly halfway between St. Augustine and Pensacola, the capitals of East and West Florida, respectively. Following the forced removal of Native Americans in 1830, Tallahassee became the heart of the Cotton Belt and the center of Florida's slave trade.

1.13 Tallahassee Courthouse, Tallassee, Florida, exterior view. The four-story granite and limestone courthouse, which combines Beaux-Arts and Neoclassical styles, was funded by the Works Progress Administration and designed by Eric Kebbon. *Photograph by Cliff Watson, courtesy of the author.*

Tallahassee's federal courthouse, which originally housed its post office, was built in 1935–36 (fig. 1.13). A Works Progress Administration building, it was designed by Eric Kebbon, an architect with the Section responsible for more than one hundred public schools. He was also well known for his work on the Food Building at the 1939 New York World's Fair. The four-elevation, granite and limestone courthouse combines Beaux-Arts and Neoclassical styles and features round arched windows with limestone keystones on the ground level and Tuscan columns and a limestone balustrade on the second floor. It has a copper roof adorned with a cornice and limestone cupola. The interior features marble flooring and wainscoting, marble pilasters, decorative crown molding, and bronze ornaments and grills. The lobby's original brass light fixtures with frosted glass globes still hang today.

Ulreich's murals, which measure 8'x4' each, hang just beneath the crown molding on the north wall of the lobby (fig. 1.14). Completed in 1939, they present viewers with a narrative history of Florida painted in a modern, naturalistic style. Rather than holding a contest for the commission, the Section selected well-known artist Eduard "Buk" Ulreich for the project based on the merits of his previous work. Born in Koszeg, Austria-Hungary, in 1884, Ulreich immigrated to the United States in 1889. He studied at the Kansas

City Art Institute and the Pennsylvania Academy of the Fine Arts and was well known for his magazine illustrations and murals. His advertisements for Dole Pineapple Juice were published in *Ladies' Home Companion*, and he designed and painted *Wild West*, a mural for Radio City Music Hall. He also created marble mosaics for the 1933 Century of Progress Exhibition in Chicago and developed the iconography used in the murals created for the U.S. Pavilion at the International Exposition of Art and Technology in Modern Life held in Paris in 1937. In addition to *History of Florida*, for which he was paid $3,500, he was commissioned by the Section to paint *Advance Guard of the West* for the post office in New Rockford, North Dakota (1940), and *Indians Watching Stagecoach in the Distance* and *Pony Express* for the post office in Columbus, Missouri (1937).

Ulreich is notable for his attention to Native American themes, a predilection he attributed to his work as a cowboy on the Pine Ridge Indian Reservation (Oglala Lakota) in South Dakota and the Fort Apache Indian Reservation (White Mountain Apache) in Arizona when he was in his twenties. Ulreich characterized his time on reservations as a young man as an important opportunity for artistic study, and many of his compositions include representations of Indigenous peoples.

1.11 Tallahassee Courthouse lobby, installation view of Ulreich's murals. The lobby features marble flooring and wainscoting, marble pilasters, decorative crown molding and bronze ornamentation. *Photograph by Cliff Watson, courtesy of the author.*

Ulreich received his contract for the Tallahassee murals from the Section in December 1941 and was given 520 days to complete the murals. His eight-panel cycle for the post office and courthouse in Tallahassee evidences his interest in Native Americans. It begins with pre-contact scenes of Indigenous peoples and concludes with an image of tourism and leisure in contemporary Florida. The first painting in the *History of Florida* (1939) cycle, which the federal General Services Administration (GSA) named *Five Standards on Parade* (fig. 1.15), shows the flags of the five nations—Spain, France, Great Britain, the United States of America, and the Confederate States of America—that have flown over Florida over the course of its history. The Section rejected Ulreich's first sketch of the flags, instructing him to render them more accurately. After extensive study of the state's seals, he resubmitted his drawing to the Section, which accepted his revision.

The second panel in the cycle (Plate 7), which Ulreich described as "Primitive Florida before the arrival of the white man" and the General Services Administration named *Aborigine*, shows pre-contact Indigenous peoples fishing and trading. Muskogean-speaking people were in North Florida as early as 1200 CE, and Native Americans of the Mississippian Culture built mounds in the area. The Lake Jackson Archaeological Site is the largest known ceremonial complex in North Florida and dates to the Fort Walton period (1000–1450 CE), but Ulreich's mural doesn't make direct reference to the Mississippian Culture site or its artifacts. Instead, Ulreich's mural offers viewers a scene of pre-contact life inspired by his knowledge of Native life gleaned from his time in the West and through his study at museums in New York and Washington, D.C. The central figure, adorned with face paint, five eagle feathers, shell necklaces, a large gold pendant, and a long black-and-white mantle, appears to be a chief or leader. Ulreich may have borrowed the central figure's posture from Horatio Greenough's statue *Enthroned Washington* (1832), which was inspired by Phidias's Statue of Zeus at Olympia, one of the Seven Wonders of the Ancient World destroyed in late antiquity. The central figure holds a mace in one hand and lifts a fringed bag with the other. To the right of him, a man with a mohawk (a hairstyle worn by some warriors of the Pawnee, Algonquian, Mohegan, and Lenape) in a loincloth and face paint holds up a large fish. Behind him a nude woman scrapes a pot while a young child plays behind her. In the distance behind them others are shown rowing two-person canoes in a body of water, perhaps Lake Jackson. To the left of the chief, two more men, identified as warriors by their large gorgets, are visible. One crouches in the stance of an archer, while the second holds a spear and a shield.

1.15 Eduard "Buk" Ulreich, *Five Standards on Parade, History of Florida*, 1939. Oil on canvas, 12' x 4'. US Courthouse, Tallahassee, Florida. *Photograph by Cliff Watson, courtesy of the author.*

The warrior's shield is incised with the design of the Castalian Springs Mississippian Gorget (1250–1350 CE). Found in 1891 in Sumner County, Tennessee, the Castalian Springs Mississippian Gorget is the most famous shell gorget ever discovered in the Southeast. Carved from whelk, it was found in a funereal mound and depicts a young warrior dancing in imitation of the Morning Star (Venus), a symbol of masculinity. The severed head in the dancer's right hand attests to his warrior status. He wears a red roached headdress that imitates the crest of a woodpecker, also a symbol of the Morning Star. The copper ornament pinned through the hair at the back of his head symbolizes the spear-thrower, and the eye pattern on his face suggests a hawk, symbolizing "swift pursuit and unerring aim." The flint mace in the dancer's left hand often was painted half red for the Morning Star and half white for the corresponding female deity, the Evening Star.

The Castalian Springs Mississippian Gorget was excavated by special archaeologist for the Smithsonian Institution's Bureau of American Ethnology William E. Myer and entered the collection of the Museum of the American Indian in New York in 1926, where Ulreich may have seen it. Although the actual object is just shy of four inches in diameter and as a gorget would have been worn around the neck, Ulreich enlarged the design and depicted it on a shield so viewers of the mural can easily decipher it from a distance.

Curvilinear lines, a palette of soft roses and blues, and abstract patterns create separate spheres in which the figures appear to float. Interspersed around them, Ulreich has included stylized depictions of native flora and fauna, including hibiscus, palms, and cacti; gulls, herons, and bears; an eagle, a dog, a gopher, a flamingo, a butterfly, a rabbit, and a deer. Ulreich's style is both detailed and whimsical, and he has employed multiple perspectives and stylized naturalism to create lively vignettes. Anthropological details date the setting of the scene to the middle Mississippian period, 1100–1350, and the scene mythologizes the fecundity of the land and the bravery of the Muskogean-speaking peoples pre-contact. While this mural depicts a scene of Indigenous life before European occupation, the rest of the murals in Ulreich's cycle depict scenes that occurred under various conquering nations' flags.

The third mural (Plate 8), which Ulreich described in his notes as "Ponce de Leon, a symbolic figure in full armor, discovering the land of flowers," and the General Services Administration titles simply *Juan Ponce de Leon*, depicts Spanish explorer Juan Ponce de León (1474–1521), who, in 1493, at the age of nineteen, secured a position on Christopher Columbus's second voyage to the Caribbean. After serving as governor of Puerto Rico, he embarked on an exploration in 1513 of a territory to the north, which he named La Florida. Searching for the Fountain of Youth, which was said to be on the island of Bimini (Bimini is the westernmost district of the Bahamas and comprises a chain of islands located fifty miles east of Miami), Ponce de León is depicted as a conquistador on horseback carrying a large cross, horn, and sword. A putto holds a banner of honor above him as he charges bravely across the canvas. Behind him are ships flying under the Spanish flag; before him lies a utopic garden and large fountain. The composition is simple and dynamic, featuring large areas of bold color that render the narrative legible from a distance. Despite Ponce de León's optimism in the mural, his attempt to secure a settlement in southern Florida was met with resistance by the Native Calusa inhabitants, and during a military conflict, he was fatally wounded. Initially, his body was buried in a crypt at San Jose Cathedral (his familial church), but in 1908 it was transferred to the Metropolitan Cathedral of San Juan Bautista in recognition of his role in establishing Puerto Rico as a successful Spanish colony.

The fourth panel (Plate 9), which Ulreich called "DeSoto discovering Indian Village where Tallahassee now is" and the GSA calls *Suturibo* [*sic*] *and Ludonniere* [*sic*], depicts the Timucuan chief Saturiwa welcoming René Goulaine de Laudonnière, a French Huguenot explorer and founder of the French colony at Fort Caroline. Laudonnière and his men landed in present-day St. Augustine in 1565. Behind Laudonnière, four soldiers, French flags, and a ship are visible. Chief Saturiwa, who was a prominent figure and ruler of thirty Timucuan-speaking villages along the St. Johns River, is depicted wearing a large spotted conch shell headdress and offering Laudonnière a peace pipe. The warriors behind him dance while holding feathers and rattles. Three women carry platters of food. When Jean Ribault first explored La Florida in 1562, he erected a column bearing the coat of arms of the queen of France. The column is depicted between Chief Saturiwa and Laudonnière. Ulreich has continued his use of multiple perspectives, stylized details, and naturalistic figures. This, combined with the use of a complementary color palette, helps connect the murals in the cycle.

The fifth panel (fig. 1.16), called "Battle of English and Spanish for possession" by Ulreich and named *Sir Francis Drake* by the GSA, depicts the English privateer in his ship across from the Spanish watchtower at St. Augustine. Drake, knowing that Governor Pedro Menéndez de Márquez ordered the massacre of all the French Huguenots who had settled in the area, fired on the town on June 6, 1586, avenging his fellow Protestants and forcing the governor and his people to flee. The English garrisoned the town and razed it to the ground. The buildings, including the Fort of San Juan, were torched and the crops destroyed, to the embarrassment of King Philip II, who ordered the Spanish to return to the area and build an impenetrable fort. Ulreich employed lavish blues and pinks to depict Drake aboard his ship watching the city burn.

The settler colonial history of La Florida continues with the sixth panel (Plate 10), which Ulreich called "Andrew Jackson," and the GSA refers to as *General Andrew Jackson*. It depicts a mounted Jackson beneath a large unfurling U.S. flag, riding away from the First Seminole War. When Chief Neamathla refused Jackson's orders to relocate, Jackson responded by burning the Native village to the ground. The Mvskoke (Muscogee) retaliated, killing fifty soldiers and civilians, but Jackson reentered Florida in March 1818 and marched down the Apalachicola River, burning more than three hundred Native homes along the way. Jackson then turned south, reaching St. Marks on April 6, 1818. He is shown riding confidently toward the viewer as behind him the walls of the new Fort Gadsden are erected. Following the war, Jackson was named the governor of the new Florida Territory, and Tallahassee became the capital when it was chosen because it was roughly halfway between St. Augustine and Pensacola.

The seventh panel (fig. 1.17), which Ulreich called "The Indian Chief Osceola" and the GSA simply named *Osceola*, depicts the 1834 peace negotiation between Seminole chief Osceola and territorial representative José Hernandez. Osceola was a celebrity in his own time, arrested and imprisoned by General Thomas S. Jesup at Fort Marion (the Castillo de San

Marcos) before being transported to Fort Moultrie near Charleston, South Carolina, where he died on January 30, 1838. A calumet pipe hangs in the sky above Chief Osceola's horse Renegade. In the distance, Seminole warriors are visible. Hernandez sits beneath a curtain of honor in the uniform of a brigadier general. He holds a rolled document in one hand and a sword in the other. Behind him the rose-colored curtain is represented in abstracted folds, mimicking the lines of the soldiers' bayonets. While meeting under a flag of truce, Osceola was captured, which ignited the Second Seminole War. Ulreich emphasized the betrayal by showing the peaceful Seminole people on one side of the composition with the hidden U.S. militia on the other. Three of Ulreich's murals for the Tallahassee courthouse include representations of Native Americans, an interest he attributed to his youth, but Native life was also a favorite subject of the Section, which often encouraged artists to paint these types of scenes.

1.16 Eduard "Buk" Ulreich, *Sir Francis Drake, History of Florida*, 1939. Oil on canvas, 12' x 4'. U.S. Courthouse, Tallahassee, Florida. *Photograph by Cliff Watson, courtesy of the author.*

The final panel in the cycle (fig. 1.18), which Ulreich called "Modern Florida, and what it is to the rest of the United States" and the GSA identifies as *Florida Today*, depicts an idealized view of Florida in the late 1930s. Contemporary men and women in the latest fashions are shown at leisure, playing golf, practicing archery, fishing, bicycling, horseback riding, and sailing. Ulreich also includes a 1939 Hudson, perhaps an acknowledgment of the ways in which automobiles were transforming the nation and the state.

Ulreich's murals *Aborigine* and *Florida Today* (both peaceful, idyllic scenes) bookend the cycle, which creates a lively narrative of Florida's history. The murals are united by a similar pastel color palette accented with bold areas of black and white. Ulreich's stylized naturalism is pleasant and his color

Top: 1.17 Eduard "Buk" Ulreich, *Osceola, History of Florida*, 1939. Oil on canvas, 12' x 4'. U.S. Courthouse, Tallahassee, Florida. *Photograph by Cliff Watson, courtesy of the author.*

Bottom: 1.18 Eduard "Buk" Ulreich, *Florida Today, History of Florida*, 1939. Oil on canvas, 12' x 4'. U.S. Courthouse, Tallahassee, Florida. *Photograph by Cliff Watson, courtesy of the author.*

choices reassuring, all of which combine to create a cohesive history of the state's settlement by Indigenous and European nations. Despite the support of the Washington office—Assistant Director of the Section Edward Rowan noted that it was "unusually good"—there were criticisms from the local community. The Head of the Art Department at the Florida State College for Women (now Florida State University) found the subject matter "trite" and the figures "wooden and poorly drawn," whereas Postmaster Cochran concluded it was "entirely too gaudy and colorful," more like advertising than art. It will be interesting to see if Ulreich's murals, many of which allude to war and rely on vague generalizations in their depictions of Native Americans, will survive the current controversies.

George Snow Hill (1898–1969)

Cypress Logging, 1938

Perry Post Office
1600 South Jefferson Street
Perry, FL 32348

Follow Highway 27 fifty-files miles southeast of Tallahassee to reach Perry, the "Tree Capital of the South." Known for its lucrative lumber industry, Perry was originally named Rosehead for the many wild roses found in the area, but in 1875, its name was changed to Perrytown, after Florida's fourth governor and former Confederate colonel Madison Stark Perry. Within a few short years, it would become known simply as Perry, the only incorporated city in Taylor County in 1903.

By 1892, yellow pine and southern bald cypress felled in North Florida and exported to the North totaled 100 million feet annually, and between 1910 and 1920 the population of Perry nearly doubled to support the lumber industry. Despite the general prosperity of the 1920s for middle-class Americans, the rapid social and economic changes of the decade also fostered increased racism and nativism. The anti-immigration movement contributed to the rise of the Ku Klux Klan in Florida, with violence erupting in Rosewood, Ocoee, and Perry in the early 1920s. In December 1922, in retaliation for the murder of Ruby Hendry, a White female schoolteacher, a mob in Perry killed four Black men and destroyed several buildings in Perry's Black community.

Florida resident George Snow Hill was invited to submit sketches for the Spanish Colonial Revival–style post office in Perry (fig. 1.19) based on designs he had previously submitted for consideration in the contest to paint murals for the Miami Courthouse. Hill had studied at Syracuse University and lived in Paris for six years, exhibiting regularly throughout Europe. The first two drawings he submitted for consideration for the Perry Post Office were "From Tree to Mail" and "Letters of Life," but these were rejected by the Section, which feared they were "boring" in the first case and "overly complex" in the second. Looking to find a more appropriate topic, Hill visited Perry to meet the postmaster and the editor of the local newspaper. On learning that Perry boasted the largest cypress logging mill in the world, he decided the lumber industry would make the most compelling subject for the post office mural. Although the vast

Top: 1.19 Old Perry Post Office, Perry, Florida, 2009. Built in 1935 with Treasury Department funds, the historic post office was sponsored by the federal Public Works Administration. It is the only PWA project undertaken in Taylor County. Today it is an administrative building for the county. *Photograph by Ebyabe, courtesy of Wikipedia Commons.*

Bottom: 1.20 George Snow Hill, *Cypress Logging* (mural study, Perry, Florida Post Office), circa 1938, oil on fiberboard, 7½" x 22" (19.0 x 55.9 cm). *Smithsonian American Art Museum, Transfer from the Internal Revenue Service through the General Services Administration, 1962.8.65.*

virgin pine and cypress forests that had covered north Florida were nearly depleted by 1930, Hill worked up his design (fig. 1.20), which was approved by the Section in May 1937. The review board noted, "The color is quite charming, the spatial quality behind the trees and beyond are very good and there are interesting parts in the foreground such as men working." Hill was given 180 days to complete the mural (Plate 11), which elides any contemporary racism or the then recent massacre by depicting eight White and two Black men chopping down trees and using cranes and pulleys to load cypress logs onto a rail car. Installed in February 1938, the mural is a particularly modern scene that pays homage to the importance of timber and the railroad to Florida's development. Its strong verticals and use of bright colors make for a dynamic scene that was clearly influenced by both the Precisionist art movement and modern photography.

GEORGE SNOW HILL (1898–1969)

Long Staple Cotton, 1940

MADISON POST OFFICE
197 SOUTHWEST PINCKNEY STREET
MADISON, FL 32340

Thirty-two miles northeast of Perry, you'll find Madison. The largest town in the then largest county in the state, Madison was named for Madison C. Livingston, who donated the first parcel of land to create the city in 1838. Madison was home to the world's largest long staple cotton gin (fig. 1.21) until the boll weevil arrived in 1916 and wiped out the cotton industry—after this, the gin's steam engine was used to process peanuts. In the center of Madison is the Wardlaw-Smith-Goza House, an antebellum mansion that dates to 1860 and served as a Confederate hospital during the Civil War. North Florida, with its strong associations to antebellum slavery, shifted to tenancy and sharecropping after the war to produce cotton, tobacco, and peanuts.

Madison's Treasury-funded Public Works Administration post office (fig. 1.22) was built in 1936, with the cornerstone (fig. 1.23) laid under the authority of supervising architect Louis A. Simon. An early execution of the standard plan, the Madison Post Office lacks much in the way of ornamentation. The red brick building features a flat façade with a fan window above the double doors. Two rectangular windows frame each side of the door, which is reached by a half flight of stairs. Originally, sculptor Constance Ortmayer was commissioned to carve a relief panel to decorate the new building, but the Section reassigned her to the Arcadia Post Office in Central Florida. Just off the success of the Perry Post Office, George Snow Hill was offered the project on June 6, 1938. His sketches were accepted without competition, and he was given eight months and $1,200 to complete the mural.

1.21 Madison steam engine, Madison, Florida. The Florida Manufacturing Company steam engine was used in cotton and peanut processing until 1919. The company operated from 1874 until it was acquired by J&P Coats in 1890. The plant closed in 1916. *Photograph by Cliff Watson, courtesy of the author.*

1.22 Madison Post Office, Madison, Florida. This Treasury Department–funded Public Works Administration post office was built in 1936 under supervising architect Louis A. Simon. *Photograph by Cliff Watson, courtesy of the author.*

1.23 Madison Post Office cornerstone, Madison, Florida. The Madison Post Office cornerstone was laid in 1936 under the direction of Secretary of the Treasury Henry Morgenthau Jr. Louis A. Simon was the architect and Neal A. Melick the engineer. *Photograph by Cliff Watson, courtesy of the author.*

Although Madison is just thirty miles from Perry, Hill found the towns strikingly dissimilar, and although the Perry postmaster was interested in the timber industry—and Hill had proven his interest in the subject—the postmaster in Madison enthusiastically supported a mural that celebrated the town's agrarian roots. Hill was taken on a tour of a cotton plantation on the Sewanee River and was so impressed with the scenery that he planned to return to Madison in September to watch the harvest. Hill submitted his preliminary sketch to the Section in October 1938 and described the mural in language that reveals the racialized nature of the cotton industry:

The interior is that of the long staple Cotton gin which I sketched at Madison, and which is one of the oldest in the South. It represents the main floor of the gin, and the half loft above to which the cotton is first blown through the large blower pipe which takes it from the cars and trucks or from the storage bins. From this half loft the colored boys push it to openings of the various shutes through which it drops or is fed to the gins below. This half loft is lighted by a sky light in the roof and provides a very interesting light on the perspiring boys.

Hill installed *Long Staple Cotton* (Plate 12) on November 11, 1940. It is a contemporary scene, but it recalls the past, depicting twelve Black men and one Black youth working in a cotton gin. The scene also includes a White man in a 1930s-era suit and fedora holding a clipboard. Beyond the gin, Hill included a cotton field where more workers are depicted stooping over cotton plants. The Wardlaw-Smith-Goza plantation house is visible in the distance. Although the painting idealizes the continuation of the plantation system in the twentieth century, Assistant Director of the Section Edward Rowan wrote in length about the success of the design, citing Hill's strong use of single-point perspective and his choice of the central figure to tie the composition together.

Like *Cypress Logging*, *Long Staple Cotton* provides viewers with a detailed look at the machinery of the gin—its feeders, dryers, cylinder cleaners, extractors, rollers, and balers—and the men who make it all run. The strong verticals of the men, the pillars, and the pipes contrast with the horizontals created by the flooring, siding, and stairs. Added to this geometric composition is the diagonals of the ropes, pulleys, and furrowed fields. Taken together, these elements create an energetic scene of modern labor and industry at a time when unemployment was high and cotton production low.

On August 18, 2020, the *Madison County Carrier* reported that Hill's mural had been covered with black plastic sheeting, saying, "Hill's work has come under fire in recent years because the workers depicted in his paintings are African-Americans [*sic*]." The article goes on to say, "The local Postmaster, Erica Carmichael, was unavailable for comment on the reasons for the painting being covered. The clerks working in the post office also made no comment on the painting. Greene Publishing, Inc. reached out to Tom Billington, District Manager for the Gulf Atlantic District (which covers Madison) of the U.S. Postal Service, but he was unavailable for comment."

The fate of this mural and others like it that have been recently covered remains to be seen. Although it is not a scene of enslavement, it is one of tenancy, which, "like slavery," as noted by historian John Michael Vlach, "proved to be an onerous system of indenture characterized by coercion, fear, and violence." The mural idealizes the southern agricultural economy, one that, as argued by novelist Erskine Caldwell in 1937, "has been wringing the blood and marrow from the South for two hundred years."

PIETRO LAZZARI (1895–1979)

Harvest at Home, 1942
News from Afar, 1942

JASPER POST OFFICE
105 SOUTHEAST MARTIN LUTHER KING DRIVE
JASPER, FL 32052

From Madison head thirty miles due east to your next stop, Jasper. The Treaty of Moultrie Creek displaced the Native Muskogean-speaking people who lived in the area to a reservation in the center of the peninsula and opened the land that would become Jasper to White settlement in 1823. In 1865, the Savannah, Florida, and Western Railway built a depot a mile north of Jasper's town center, and the town grew steadily between 1890 and 1930 due to its trade in turpentine, tobacco, cotton, and pine lumber. By the 1920s, Jasper's population was at its height, boasting more than two thousand people.

The Section invited Pietro Lazzari to paint murals for the Jasper Post Office in 1941. A muralist, sculptor, and educator, Lazzari was born in Rome in 1898. He was associated with the Futurists and, after serving in World War I, studied at the Ornamental School of Rome before moving to the United States in 1929. Lazzari visited Jasper in late 1941 and returned in 1942 to complete the murals. The Section approved his cartoons on April 20, 1942.

Lazzari's two murals, *Harvest at Home* (Plate 13) and *News from Afar* (Plate 14), unlike the other oil on canvas murals that hang in Florida's post offices, were painted in tempera directly on the post office's walls. Although Lazzari had worked with the Futurists (known for their paintings that emphasized speed, technology, and youth), these murals offer a naturalistic, even folksy, portrayal of the town's history and industry. *Harvest at Home* depicts White and Black men laboring, getting turpentine from pine trees; hoeing, picking, and drying tobacco; and sawing logs. *News from Afar* pictures a couple with a baby in a cradle receiving their mail while an older man sits whittling behind them. In the center, a mailman in a horse-drawn carriage delivers a letter to a woman. At the right, a man carries a bucket after milking a cow. Unlike George Snow Hill's modernist scenes set in 1930s Florida, Lazzari opted for nostalgic scenes of the territory's pioneers. Inspired by stereotypical descriptions of Floridians such as those published in the *New York Times* that described "Crackers swing[ing] their partners in squares on Saturdays, sometimes in a schoolhouse, sometimes in a rustic pavilion," Lazzari presents viewers with scenes of an idealized past. For many, by the late 1930s, the Florida Cracker had come to represent a rejection of the commercialized, tropical Florida prevalent in the popular media, and Lazzari's mural may be interpreted as offering contemporary viewers a romanticized past that evoked an alternative to the tropical picture of Florida promoted by chambers of commerce, roadside attractions, and Florida Park Service brochures.

Lazzari appears to have appreciated undeveloped Florida, writing to Assistant Director Edward Rowan, "I like Jasper and the warmth of its rural and dusty roads. I discussed plans for the decoration with the Postmaster, Mr. Kirby Sandlin and I am entirely confident of his cooperation. The place is exciting and I am returning before the end of this week to take up residence in Jasper." Postmaster Sandlin was equally impressed with Lazzari, writing, "Your paintings I think are excellent and the blending of the colors are wonderful and the thoughts that are conveyed by the paintings are so plain that they could be caught at once even by a novice."

After completing the project, Lazzari left New York City, moving to Washington, D.C., where he taught painting and sculpture at American University before becoming the chair of the Art Department at Dumbarton College. In addition to the two murals he painted for the Jasper Post Office, Lazzari created *Good News* for the Transylvania Public Library in Brevard, North Carolina (1941). Though he never returned to Jasper, he did value his work for the Section, later recalling, "The art renaissance in America was born under the Roosevelt administration. The WPA (Works Progress Administration) and federal competitions sponsored by the Public Works of Art Project brought to artists in this country a new freedom and independence. I was part of this wonderful renaissance, which let the artist create freely and be happy." Thousands of artists like Lazzari were employed by New Deal programs, saving them from poverty and enabling Americans across the nation to enjoy original works of art, evidence of creativity during a time of tremendous economic upheaval.

O'LENO STATE PARK

410 SOUTHEAST OLENO PARK ROAD
HIGH SPRINGS, FL 32643

Head south on I-75 from the Jasper Post Office for fifty miles and you'll find O'Leno State Park. Built on the site of one of Florida's original ghost towns, Leno was established in the mid-nineteenth century along the banks of the Santa Fe River. Originally named Keno after the poker game, it was renamed Leno in 1876 to obscure the reference to gambling. Leno was an industrious town with two gristmills, a sawmill, and six cotton gins, but when the railroad was built through neighboring Fort White, the town fell on hard times. By 1896, everyone had moved away.

The natural landscape of O'Leno State Park is marked by a mix of upland woodlands of pop ash, green haw, swamp laurel oak, winged elm, water locust, and bluff oak. Initially chosen as the site of a Florida Forest Service camp, O'Leno was developed by the Works Progress Administration before the Civilian Conservation Corps installed workers there in July 1935. Between 1933 and 1938 the Works Progress Administration and Civilian Conservation Corps cleared land, built roads and trails, and constructed buildings for the park (fig. 1.24). In 1938, O'Leno opened as a Forest Service camp to train employees and youth groups interested in forestry. The Forestry Service ran the camp for two summers before turning the camp over to the Florida Park Service, which opened it as a state park in 1940. Its only employee, Carlos Maxwell, was named the park's first superintendent.

O'Leno State Park is an excellent example of a karst, or landscape where the dissolution of bedrock creates sinkholes, sinking streams, caves, and

1.24 The mess hall at O'Leno State Park, High Springs, Florida, circa 1940. General Collection, Florida Memory Project. *Courtesy of the State Archives of Florida.*

springs. Its most notable feature is the Sinking Creek Bridge (Plate 15), a suspension bridge built by the Civilian Conservation Corps that spans the Santa Fe River. A tributary of the Suwannee River, the Santa Fe is a disappearing river that runs underground at the park's river sink. The park also features trails, sinkholes, hardwood hammocks, river swamps, and sandhills and provides habitat for threatened and endangered species such as the gopher tortoise, indigo snake, and sand skink. Today, you can camp at O'Leno in cabins built by the Civilian Conservation Corps, visit the Civilian Conservation Corps Museum on site, launch a kayak from the banks of the Santa Fe River, go for a swim, or enjoy a picnic lunch in a Civilian Conservation Corps–built pavilion.

ELIZABETH TERRELL (1908–1993)

Reforestation, 1942 (Destroyed)

STARKE POST OFFICE
122 NORTH WALNUT STREET
STARKE, FL 32091

From O'Leno State Park, head east thirty-five miles to find the Starke Post Office (fig. 1.25), which once housed Elizabeth Terrell's mural *Reforestation*. Unfortunately, the mural was destroyed in the 1980s during a renovation of the office's lobby and the mural survives today only in black-and-white photographs of the sketch Terrell submitted to the Section in 1942 (fig. 1.26).

Born in Toledo, Ohio, in 1908, Terrell was a New York–based artist who studied at the Arts Students League and was a member of the Woodstock Art Association. She was invited to submit a design for the post office by the Section based on the strength of *The Ploughman*, a mural she completed for the post office in Conyers, Georgia, which was selected for the "48 States" Contest.

The Section offered Terrell $700 for the 12'x5'6" mural. She researched the area and wrote to Postmaster Edward F. Strump to propose a mural about the turpentine industry. Strump replied that he liked the idea but that perhaps reforestation or conservation might make for a more interesting and timelier theme. Prior to 1857, the area around Starke was a dense forest of virgin pine, but the development of the Fernandina to Cedar Key railroad,

1.25 Exterior view of the Starke Post Office, Starke, Florida. Built in 1941 with federal funds, the post office is still in use today. *Photograph by Michael Rivera, courtesy of Wikipedia Commons.*

which connected the Atlantic Ocean to the Gulf of Mexico, brought settlers to the area. During the 1880s and 1890s, timber and oranges emerged as the area's two most important commodities, but during the 1930s significant reforestation efforts began. Terrell submitted a design for a reforestation scene to the Section, which found it "entertaining and handsome in color and approach." Terrell's plan was almost stymied, however, when Sol Swarz, a cadet stationed at nearby Camp Blanding, wrote to the national office to say that he felt a military scene by a local would be more appropriate than a design submitted by a New Yorker. Assistant Director Rowan shared the letter with Terrell, who replied that the postmaster supported her design, which she felt was more befitting the community. She was permitted to continue her work, and a sketch in the National Archives reveals Terrell's design. It features two men and a teenage boy in the foreground. The older man on the far right uses a pickaxe to break down a tree stump and stoke a fire. Behind him the boy carries a shovel and pitchfork over his shoulder. To the right, a middle-aged man plants a seedling. In the background two deer survey the scene from a stand of pines.

Although the mural is not extant, Starke is an interesting hamlet, worth a visit. It was incorporated in 1870, making it one of the oldest communities in north-central Florida. Starke's rail station is the halfway point on Florida's first railroad, the Fernandina to Cedar Key line, and the town serves as the seat of Bradford County. Located less than an hour from Jacksonville, Starke

1.26 Elizabeth Terrell, *Reforestation*, 1942. Sketch submitted to the Treasury Section. *Courtesy of the National Archives.*

features a historic downtown with a 1940s-era movie theater. You can also catch a minor-league baseball game and cheer on the Bradford Tornadoes while you're there.

MIKE ROESS GOLD HEAD BRANCH STATE PARK

6239 STATE ROAD 21
KEYSTONE HEIGHTS, FL 32656

Just twenty minutes east of the Starke Post Office, you'll find Mike Roess Gold Head Branch State Park, so named because the initial property for the park was donated by Martin J. "Mike" Roess and is located adjacent to the Gold Head Branch, a crystal-clear stream that originates from the springs that flow beneath the park's ravines. The park is also home to one of Florida's oldest lakes, the twenty-four-thousand-year-old Sheeler Lake (Plate 16). Mike Roess Gold Head Branch State Park is characterized by a system of springs, steep ravines, and sinkhole lakes, accented by rolling sandhill and sand pine scrub plant communities. Located on the north end of Florida's central ridge, Mike Roess Gold Head Branch State Park has one of the few remaining forests of old-growth longleaf pines in the state.

Longleaf pine woodlands are the most biologically diverse environments in North America. The dominant canopy tree species in the mesic flatwoods of North Florida, longleaf pines, the largest of which are more than 350 years old, comprise 25 percent of the park. These old-growth longleaf trees typically have red heart disease, and many bear catface scars from when they were tapped for turpentine in the early twentieth century.

The Civilian Conservation Corps developed the 1,080-acre site, constructing park facilities such as roads, trails, bridges, picnic areas, and buildings and shaping the park's layout to increase its accessibility for visitors. As one Civilian Conservation Corps enrollee at Mike Roess Gold Head Branch State Park wrote in the camp newspaper, "[The park was] carved out of the wilderness." Indeed, the Civilian Conservation Corps implemented erosion-control measures such as terracing to protect the park's natural resources and prevent soil erosion, planted trees, and landscaped the park to enhance its beauty and conserve its local ecosystem. As the *WPA Guide to Florida* notes in its description of Mike Roess Gold Head Branch State Park, "The gorge is a natural garden, overspread with wildflowers, shrubs, palms, and other subtropical growth."

While visiting Mike Roess Gold Head Branch State Park, you will find historical markers and interpretive displays that provide information about the role of the Civilian Conservation Corps in the park's development. Many of the structures and improvements made by Civilian Conservation Corps members can still be seen and enjoyed by visitors today, including lakefront cabins. Part of the Florida National Scenic Trail, Mike Roess Gold Head Branch State Park was advertised in early Florida Park Service brochures as a "sportsman's paradise," and it is ideal for fishing, boating, and camping. Marjory Stoneman Douglas added a bit of exoticism to the park's description in the 1937 edition of *Parks and Playgrounds of Florida*, when she wrote that it

1.27 Civilian Conservation Corps–built rental cabin at Gold Head Branch State Park, Keystone Heights, Florida, circa 1950. Florida Park Service Collection, Florida Memory Project. *Courtesy of the State Archives of Florida.*

was full of "beautiful palms, a great variety of flowers and shrubs and trees of a subtropical nature." Many of these subtropical specimens were planted by the Civilian Conservation Corps.

RAVINE GARDENS STATE PARK

1600 TWIGG STREET
PALATKA, FL 32177

Drive southeast another thirty miles and you'll find yourself at Ravine Gardens State Park, another of Florida's New Deal–era state parks. In 1933, the Works Progress Administration put unemployed Floridians to work carving a formal botanical garden out of a steep ravine near the St. Johns River. Created to increase recreation and tourism during the Great Depression, Ravine Gardens State Park is characterized by its extensive flower garden, and unlike other New Deal parks, it is really more akin to a manicured urban park. Offering a unique cultural landscape, it fuses features of both a roadside attraction and a natural park.

Florida's leaders saw the commodification of the state's natural resources as key to tourism. A 1934 report by the Florida State Planning Board noted, "There is no better way to conserve and expand the tourist industry than by increasing the State's facilities for the entertainment of winter visitors. Well-kept forests and the beautiful clear streams and lakes of the State have scenic value as well as a recreation value." Florida existed in the national imagination as "tropical, exotic, safe, and natural," but this was an image that required work to achieve. As such, those hired by the Works Progress Administration, Civil Works Administration, and Civilian Conservation Corps often were directed to remove native fauna and flora, reroute rivers and streams, and enhance the natural landscape by planting non-native specimens. A particularly exaggerated example of this type of work is found at Ravine Gardens State Park, where workers with the WPA and CWA planted 250,000 ornamental plants and 95,000 azaleas on the park's fifty-nine acres, built cypress enclosures, and added rock gardens and fieldstone terraces (Plate 17). The Civilian Conservation Corps built the grand stairway and terraces out of native stone (fig. 1.28) and erected a gazebo in 1938 for the Miss Azalea Pageant. The Corps also paved a 1.8-mile scenic loop to provide dramatic views of the ravines and gardens, built covered picnic

1.28 Ravine Gardens State Park, Palatka, Florida, circa 1940. Postcard Collection, Florida Memory Project. *Courtesy of the State Archives of Florida.*

areas, and added two suspension bridges to cross the park's 120-foot-deep ravines. Dubbed the "Nation's Outstanding Works Administration Project," Ravine Gardens was a major tourist attraction during the 1930s and 1940s. Visit between January and March to see the azaleas in a rolling bloom.

When visiting today, you enter through a set of formal gardens, but recent conservation efforts have worked to ensure the sustainability of the natural hardwood forests of loblolly pines, as well as the freshwater marshes and ravines filled with wild irises that also mark the natural landscape of the park.

FORT CLINCH STATE PARK

2601 ATLANTIC AVENUE
FERNANDINA BEACH, FL 32034

Some 100 miles north of Ravine Gardens State Park and 120 miles east of the Jasper Post Office, you'll find Fort Clinch State Park, a 1,400-acre historical and natural environment on the northern shore of Amelia Island

(Plate 18). Once an active port, Fernandina Beach was an industrial city known for its shrimp and shad fisheries and paper pulp mills in the 1930s.

Fort Clinch State Park was established in 1935 and formally opened to the public on November 16, 1940, after its structures were restored by the Civilian Conservation Corps. In 1941, Civilian Conservation Corps veteran M.B. Greene became the park's first superintendent, and today, Fort Clinch State Park offers visitors tours of its Civil War–era fortifications (fig. 1.29), provides interpretive programs, and hosts living history programs and reenactments. If you visit on the first weekend of the month, a soldier garrison fires cannons and demonstrates battlefield skills. (If you visit on the first weekend in November, you also can attend the Right Whale Festival, which celebrates the annual return of endangered North Atlantic Right Whales to the warm coastal waters off northeast Florida to give birth and nurse their young.) In addition to the historical structures, the park has hiking trails, picnic areas, and views of the ocean (fig. 1.30). You can even see the nearby Amelia Island Lighthouse (fig. 1.31), which was built between 1838 and 1839 and is the oldest lighthouse in Florida.

The park's original master plan called for planting native grasses on the dunes and constructing bulkheads to control beach erosion, and from 1937 to 1939 the Civilian Conservation Corps worked to stabilize the shoreline and protect the fort from rising sea levels. The plan also included designs for cabins, a casino, a recreational trailer camp, overlook structures, entrance gates, nature trails, fishing piers, and picnic areas, but only a few of these projects were completed before the Civilian Conservation Corps camp was deactivated. Still, several facilities built at Fort Clinch State Park by

1.29 Fort Clinch, Fernandina Beach, Florida. Built at the mouth of the St. Marys River to protect the deep-water port, Fort Clinch is one of the most well-preserved nineteenth-century forts in the country. Although no battles were fought here, it was garrisoned during both the Civil and Spanish American Wars. In addition to serving as a sentinel against invasion, Fort Clinch also protected the eastern link of Florida's only cross-state railroad. *Photograph by Cliff Watson, courtesy of the author.*

Above: 1.30 View of the Atlantic Ocean over battlements at Fort Clinch, Fernandina Beach, Florida. Fort Clinch is one in a series of masonry forts constructed between 1816 and 1867 known as the Third System of Fortifications. *Photograph by Cliff Watson, courtesy of the author.*

Left: 1.31 View of the Amelia Island Lighthouse from Fort Clinch, Fernandina Beach, Florida. Built in 1838, the Amelia Island Lighthouse is the state's oldest lighthouse and the only one from the territorial period that has survived without major rebuilding. *Photograph by Cliff Watson, courtesy of the author.*

the Civilian Conservation Corps are still in use today, including the visitor center, the riverside campground restroom, and a picnic pavilion.

The landscape of Fort Clinch State Park supports diverse ecosystems, including maritime hammocks, tidal marshes, and coastal dunes. Florida is home to some 425 bird species, roughly half the birdlife in the United States, and Fort Clinch State Park provides habitat for bald eagles; indigo and painted buntings; pileated, downy, red-bellied and redheaded woodpeckers; and red-tailed hawks. You can also spot barred owls, great horned owls, scarlet tanagers, roseate spoonbills, purple sandpipers, warblers, vireos, and wrens, among others. If you want to spend the night, Fort Clinch has sixty-nine campsites. The Amelia River tent-only campground is shaded with oaks and offers views of the St. Marys River. The Atlantic Beach campground offers recreational vehicle and tent sites surrounded by sand dunes and the ocean.

CONCLUSION

Home to seven post offices built by the Works Progress Administration and decorated with fifteen murals commissioned by the Treasury Section of Painting and Sculpture and six state parks established by the Works Progress Administration, Civil Works Administration, and Civilian Conservation Corps, North Florida has plenty to offer art, history, and nature enthusiasts. The architecture of the post offices showcases the Colonial Revival, Beaux-Arts, and Neoclassical styles, while the murals display the popularity of realism during the 1930s and attest to the importance of cotton and timber to the region. With painted representations of Chief Osceola, Andrew Jackson, Juan Ponce de León, and Francis Drake, as well as scenes of idyllic landscapes, North Florida's post office murals offer insight into the beliefs and values of both the local community and the federal government during the 1930s. North Florida's state parks conserve a variety of ecosystems from karst landscapes of sinkholes, caves, and springs to coastal dunes and tidal marshes and present visitors with physical evidence of the natural resource management objectives of the New Deal, which included planting both native and non-native species, building picnic pavilions and craftsman cottages, and blazing trails that continue to serve visitors today.

Left: 1. George Snow Hill, *Loading Pulpwood*, 1941. Oil on canvas, 13' x 3' 4". Originally for the Milton Post Office, now in the Imogene Theatre, Milton, Florida. *Photograph by Cliff Watson, courtesy of the author.*

Right: 2. Thomas Laughlin, *Scene of Town*, 1942. Oil on canvas, 12' x 5' 4". DeFuniak Springs Post Office, DeFuniak Springs, Florida. *Photograph by Cliff Watson, courtesy of the author.*

3. Cavern, Florida Caverns State Park, Marianna, Florida, n.d.
Courtesy of Florida Park Service.

4. Blue Hole Spring, Florida Caverns State Park, Marianna,
Florida, n.d. *Courtesy of Visit Florida.*

5. Civilian Conservation Corps–built Stone Bridge, Torreya State Park, Rock Bluff, Florida, 2001. *Photograph by David Nelson, courtesy of the Florida Memory Project, State Archives of Florida.*

6. Exterior of the Gregory House, Torreya State Park, Rock Bluff, Florida, n.d. *Courtesy of Florida Park Service.*

Left: 7. Eduard "Buk" Ulreich, *Aborigine, History of Florida*, 1939. Oil on canvas, 12' x 4'. U.S. Courthouse, Tallahassee, Florida. *Photograph by Cliff Watson, courtesy of the author.*

Right: 8. Eduard "Buk" Ulreich, *Juan Ponce de León*, *History of Florida*, 1939. Oil on canvas, 12' x 4'. U.S. Courthouse, Tallahassee, Florida. *Photograph by Cliff Watson, courtesy of the author.*

Left: 9. Eduard "Buk" Ulreich, *Suturibo* [sic] *and Ludonniere* [sic], *History of Florida,* 1939. Oil on canvas, 12' x 4'. U.S. Courthouse, Tallahassee, Florida. *Photograph by Cliff Watson, courtesy of the author.*

Right: 10. Eduard "Buk" Ulreich, *General Andrew Jackson, History of Florida,* 1939. Oil on canvas, 12' x 4'. U.S. Courthouse, Tallahassee, Florida. *Photograph by Cliff Watson, courtesy of the author.*

Left: 11. George Snow Hill, *Cypress Logging*, 1938. Oil on canvas, 13' x 3' 4". Perry Post Office, Perry, Florida. *Photograph by Cliff Watson, courtesy of the author.*

Right: 12. George Snow Hill, *Long Staple Cotton*, 1940. Oil on canvas. Madison Post Office, Madison, Florida. *Photograph by Cliff Watson, courtesy of the author.*

Left: 13. Pietro Lazzari, *Harvest at Home,* 1942. Oil on canvas, dimensions, Jasper Post Office, Jasper, Florida. *Photograph by Cliff Watson, courtesy of the author.*

Right: 14. Pietro Lazzari, *News from Afar*, 1942. Oil on canvas, dimensions, Jasper Post Office, Jasper, Florida. *Photograph by Cliff Watson, courtesy of the author.*

Above: 15. Civilian Conservation Corps–built Suspension Bridge, O'Leno State Park, High Springs, Florida, n.d. *Courtesy of Florida Park Service.*

Left: 16. Sheeler Lake, Mike Roess Gold State Park, Palatka, Florida, n.d. *Courtesy of Florida Park Service.*

Above: 17. Scenic view showing garden path at the Ravine State Gardens park in Palatka, Florida, circa 1941. Postcard Collection, Florida Memory Project. *Courtesy of the State Archives of Florida.*

Left: 18. Fort Clinch State Park, Fernandina Beach, Florida, 2003. *Courtesy of Wikipedia Commons.*

19. Civilian Conservation Corps–built Suspension Bridge, Hillsborough River State Park, Thonotosassa, Florida, n.d. *Courtesy of Florida Park Service.*

20. Denman Fink, *Harvest Time–Lake Wales*, 1942. Oil on canvas, 3'2" x 14'5". Lake Wales Post Office, Lake Wales, Florida. *Photograph by Cliff Watson, courtesy of the author.*

21. Civilian Conservation Corps Museum, Highlands Hammock State Park, Sebring, Florida, n.d. *Photograph by Carla Sherwin, courtesy of Florida Park Service.*

22. Charles R. Knight, *Prehistoric Life in Florida*, 1942. Oil on canvas, 4'11" x 13'1". Originally for the Sebring Post Office, now in the Public Library, Sebring, Florida. *Photograph by Cliff Watson, courtesy of the author.*

23. View of the Myakka River, n.d. *Courtesy of the Florida Park Service.*

24. Lucille Blanch, *Osceola Holding Informal Court with His Chiefs*, 1938. Oil on canvas, 4'3" x 4'11". Fort Pierce Post Office, Fort Pierce, Florida. *Photograph by Cliff Watson, courtesy of the author.*

25. Charles Rosen, *Seminole Indians*, 1938. Oil on canvas, 19'4" x 7'4". Palm Beach Post Office, Palm Beach, Florida. *Photograph by Cliff Watson, courtesy of the author.*

26. Stevan Dohanos, *Legend of James Edward Hamilton, Barefoot Mailman*, 1939. Oil on canvas, 8' by 4'. West Palm Beach Post Office, West Palm Beach, Florida. *Photograph by Cliff Watson, courtesy of the author.*

27. Stevan Dohanos, *Legend of James Edward Hamilton, Barefoot Mailman*, 1939. Oil on canvas, 8' by 4'. West Palm Beach Post Office, West Palm Beach, Florida. *Photograph by Cliff Watson, courtesy of the author.*

28. Stevan Dohanos, *Legend of James Edward Hamilton, Barefoot Mailman*, 1939. Oil on canvas, 8' by 4'. West Palm Beach Post Office, West Palm Beach, Florida. *Photograph by Cliff Watson, courtesy of the author.*

29. Stevan Dohanos, *Legend of James Edward Hamilton, Barefoot Mailman*, 1939. Oil on canvas, 8' by 4'. West Palm Beach Post Office, West Palm Beach, Florida. *Photograph by Cliff Watson, courtesy of the author.*

30. Joseph D. Myers, *Settler Fighting Alligator from Rowboat*, 1946. Oil on canvas, Lake Worth Post Office, Lake Worth, Florida. *Photograph by Cliff Watson, courtesy of the author.*

31. Denman Fink, *Law Guides Florida Progress*, 1940. Oil on canvas, 25'3" x 11'2". Miami Courthouse, Miami, Florida. *Photograph by Cliff Watson, courtesy of the author.*

32. Royal Palm Lodge, Royal Palm State Park, Homestead, Florida, circa 1900. Postcard Collection, Florida Memory Project. *Courtesy of the State Archives of Florida.*

II
CENTRAL FLORIDA

C entral Florida, as defined by the state's economic development agency and the Florida Department of Transportation, includes the greater Tampa Bay and Orlando metropolitan areas and their surrounding counties.

Two post offices and two state parks were established in Central Florida during the Great Depression. Post offices were built with funds provided by the Works Progress Administration and decorated with murals sponsored by the Treasury Section of Painting and Sculpture in Lake Wales (1940) and Sebring (1941), and state parks were constructed by the Civilian Conservation Corps in Thonotosassa (1935) and Sebring (1931). These post offices, decorative murals, and state parks attest to the rich history of Central Florida, its architecture, ecosystems, and people.

Indigenous peoples lived in the geographical area known as Central Florida for more than twelve thousand years before Europeans sailed to the Americas, and Vero Beach, Melbourne, and Helen Blazes are home to some of the continent's oldest fossils. In 1915, twenty-six fossilized human bones were found in the banks of the main canal in Vero (now Vero Beach). Dating to the Late Pleistocene Period (twenty to ten thousand years ago), these fossils include an engraved mammoth tusk and a full human skeleton. Similarly, the Melbourne Bed has yielded fossils of numerous extinct animals, including dire wolves, Florida cave bears, giant armadillos, giant beavers, giant bison, giant ground sloths, mammoths, mastodons, saber-tooth tigers, and tapirs. Prehistoric human remains and artifacts also have been found at Helen Blazes in present-day Brevard County.

Indigenous peoples lived in Florida throughout what archaeologists have named the Archaic (7500 BCE–500 BCE) and Woodland (1000 BCE–1000 CE) periods, and one of the oldest settlements in Central Florida, Ocale (now Ocala), which means "big hammock," was an important Timucua village that was occupied from 6500 BCE to the mid-1500s. Myaca and Jororo peoples lived around Lake Monroe (just north of present-day Sanford). Native Americans altered the natural landscape of Central Florida by establishing settlements, cultivating fields, building mounds, developing transportation routes, grading causeways, and digging canals and fishponds.

European explorers arrived in the 1500s, and non-Native settlement began with land grants from Spain in the seventeenth century and continued after its cession to the United States in 1821. The U.S. Army constructed Fort King in Ocala, Cape Monroe (Fort Mellon) near present-day Sanford, and Fort Gatlin in Jernigan (present-day Orlando) in the 1820s. The Treaty of Moultrie Creek in 1823 made most of Central Florida a reservation, but the Indian Removal Act of 1830 relocated many Indigenous peoples to Oklahoma and reclaimed much of the reserved land for settlement by White pioneers. Prior to statehood, Florida was covered by twenty million acres of wetlands. Today more than half of those wetlands have been ditched, drained, or filled. At the end of the Civil War, land agents and developers worked hard to attract people to the area, and early settlers from Georgia and the Carolinas homesteaded and established ranches in the prairie lands around present-day Kissimmee, St. Cloud, Orlando, and Ocala. In 1881, Hamilton Disston, a northern industrialist, purchased four million acres from the state's land trust. He straightened the Kissimmee River to Lake Okeechobee and dug a canal that connected the lake to the Caloosahatchee River (near Fort Myers) and the Gulf of Mexico. The creation of this navigable waterway allowed ships to travel along the Kissimmee River to the Gulf, transporting cattle and citrus out of Kissimmee to ports around the world. It also forever changed the drainage of the peninsula. Sanford, located at the intersection of Lake Monroe and the St. Johns River, was incorporated in 1877 as a port city. Florida also attracted artists and sportsmen. In the 1830s, John James Audubon journeyed to St. Augustine and the Keys to collect bird specimens, and in 1904, Winslow Homer spent a month fishing the Homosassa River. He was so taken by the landscape that he made seven more trips to Florida in the early twentieth century.

Florida enjoyed a land boom in the 1920s, with many lured by the promise of a "semi-tropical paradise" and cheap land advertised as well-suited for agriculture. Tourism contributed to development as well, with Henry Flagler building railroads and hotels from St. Augustine to Key West in the late nineteenth and early twentieth centuries, but major hurricanes in 1926 and 1928 thrust Florida into the Great Depression before the stock market crash of 1929. Adding insult to injury, Florida's citrus industry was devastated when the Mediterranean fruit fly invaded in 1929, reducing citrus production by 60 percent. In Florida, over ninety thousand families were affected by the Great Depression, and at the beginning of the 1930s, 25 percent of Florida's population was on some form of public relief.

During the Great Depression, as part of Roosevelt's New Deal, Congress passed the Federal Park, Parkway, and Recreational Study Act, which asked state planners to evaluate their conservation and recreation efforts and to create an inventory of properties that could be developed into parks. Funded by the Works Progress Administration, the study was completed by the Florida State Planning Board and the Florida Forestry and Parks Board between 1937 and 1939. Their research found that "climate, natural recreation, and parks" were the state's major tourist attractions, with 20 percent of people visiting the state to fish, 28 percent to sunbathe and swim, and 21 percent to sightsee. The report concluded that "the wildlife resources of Florida constitute one of the state's greatest and most valuable assets."

Despite the planning board's recognition of the economic value of the state's natural resources, marshes and swamplands were drained and diverted to improve land for agriculture, and waterways, such as canals and man-made lakes, were created for pleasure and recreation. Invasive species were introduced—in Central Florida, Rhesus macaques were brought to Silver Springs in the 1930s to increase tourism, but they decreased native bird populations, increased bacterial loads in waterways, and caused shoreline erosion—and exotic plants and fishes continue to threaten native species. Recognizing the need to both capitalize on and conserve its natural resources, the Florida Park Service, which manages Florida's state parks, was developed in 1935 with the help of the Civilian Conservation Corps, Works Progress Administration, and Civil Works Administration to set aside land for conservation and prevent overdevelopment. By the end of 1935, the Florida Park Service had acquired Florida Caverns, Torreya, Mike Roess Gold Head Branch, and Fort Clinch in North Florida; Hillsborough River and Highlands Hammock in Central Florida; and Myakka River in South Florida. Today the Florida Park Service is one of the largest and most heavily used systems in the country with 175 parks, 10 state trails, and over 800,000 acres of parkland across the state.

This section visits two state parks and two post offices constructed in Central Florida during the Great Depression. Hillsborough River State Park is just north of Tampa in Thonotosassa, and Highlands Hammock State Park is south of Orlando in Sebring. Each offers glimpses of the region's diverse natural ecosystems, which include pine flatwoods, wet prairies, temperate hardwood forests, and rocklands. Central Florida's two post offices, one in Lake Wales and the other in Sebring, present viewers with a depiction of life in prehistoric Florida and a modern scene of the landscape tamed by agricultural labor.

HILLSBOROUGH RIVER STATE PARK

15402 US-301
THONOTOSASSA, FL 33592

Just twenty miles northeast of Tampa, you'll find Hillsborough River State Park, another of Florida's original state parks. Constructed along the Hillsborough River in 1934 (fig. 2.1), the three-thousand-acre park features river rapids running through a hardwood forest.

Hillsborough River State Park was developed by the Civilian Conservation Corps, which began work there in 1934. The Civilian Conservation Corps built the caretaker's cottage, visitor cabins, administrative buildings, and bridges (Plate 19). The park's interpretive center displays a collection of more than one hundred artifacts, and reenactments of the Second Seminole War are offered twice a year in December and January (fig. 2.2). The park also includes seven miles of hiking trails, Class II river rapids (a rarity for Florida), and both full-facility and primitive camping. The park opened to the public in 1938.

As environmental historian David J. Nelson has compellingly argued, the establishment of the Florida Park Service was fraught with tension, as the goals of the federal government and the Civilian Conservation Corps often clashed with those of state politicians and local residents. Whereas federal officials and leaders of the Civilian Conservation Corps saw Florida as a tropical paradise filled with coconuts, palm trees, and flamingos, many locals considered Florida an agricultural state known for its cotton, timber, citrus, and cattle. In reality, Florida was primarily wetlands, the most biologically diverse of all ecosystems and home to a wide range of unique plant and

2.1 Hillsborough River, Hillsborough River State Park, Thonotosassa, Florida, February 24, 2008. *Photograph by Mwanner, courtesy of Wikipedia Commons.*

animal species. Florida's transition in the public imagination from a swamp to an agrarian southern state to a tropical oasis owes a debt to the New Deal and those programs—such as the Works Progress Administration, Civil Works Administration, Civilian Conservation Corps, and Treasury Section of Painting and Sculpture—that helped transform its landscape, both physically and through painted and sculptural representations, into that of a manicured Edenic paradise.

The creation and promotion of Hillsborough River State Park participated in this transformation. Part of the Green Swamp, the watershed of the Hillsborough River contains river floodplain forests, cypress domes, pine flatwoods, and sandhills, as well as oak hammocks, sawgrass marshes, hardwood swamps, and sphagnum bogs. Marketing "Florida's Jungle," Hillsborough River State Park published brochures noting the types of animals that could be seen in the river, and the park produced flyers listing its flowers, trees, and birds. Research in this area was bolstered when noted ornithologist Oscar Baynard was hired as the park's first superintendent in 1936. Having worked for the Audubon Society saving egrets from hunters in the Everglades, Baynard was eager to promote and protect the many

2.2 Seminole War reenactors at Hillsborough River State Park, Thonotosassa, Florida, November 10, 2007. *Photograph by Mwanner, courtesy of Wikipedia Commons.*

species of birds found in Hillsborough and other state parks in Florida. He published *Birds of Highlands Hammock* in 1940 and created many of the signs and interpretive materials used in both parks to this day. In 1942, botanist Carol Beck (one of the only women employed by the Florida Park Service) was hired to work alongside Baynard at Hillsborough River State Park, inventorying the park's plant and animal life, creating exhibits, and writing interpretive and didactic materials.

In addition to educational and promotional materials, the Civilian Conservation Corps erected rental cabins outfitted with "rustic furniture, electricity, water, and hand-hewn tables" and built a swinging bridge across the Hillsborough River. Crews also built picnic tables, two miles of park roads, three drinking fountains and a recreation shelter, and landscaped more than one hundred acres of the park.

Today, the park is just minutes from downtown Tampa, but it offers travelers a respite from the hustle and bustle of city life. You can stroll along the river, explore the site's historic structures built by the Civilian Conservation Corps, fish, bike, or hike. You can even "glamp" at one of the park's glamorous camp sites.

Denman Fink (1880–1956)

Harvest Time–Lake Wales, 1942

Lake Wales Post Office
6 West Park Avenue
Lake Wales, FL 33853

Fifty-five miles east of Hillsborough River State Park, you'll find Lake Wales. Established in 1911 by the Lake Wales Land Company, the town increased in popularity after the Atlantic Coast Line Railroad built a depot there in 1925 (fig. 2.3). Lake Wales is also home to Iron Mountain, one of the highest peaks on the peninsula. Inspired by its dramatic vistas, Edward W. Bok, editor of the *Ladies' Home Journal* from 1889 to 1919, purchased land there in 1923 and enlisted noted landscape architect Frederick Law Olmsted Jr., the son of Frederick Law Olmsted and a well-known landscape architect in his own right, to transform his new property into a lush garden. Over the next five years, Olmsted Jr. planted a mix of native and exotic plants, including one thousand large live oaks, ten thousand azaleas, one hundred sabal palms, three hundred magnolias, and five hundred gardenias, that reshaped the property from a sand hill into a garden sanctuary. The landscaped grounds center on Bok Tower, a sixty-bell Gothic-style carillon designed by Milton B. Medary—architect of the Washington Memorial Chapel and Detroit Institute of Arts—and sculpted by Lee O. Lawrie, well known for his works, including *Atlas* (1937), at Rockefeller Plaza. Bok Tower is built of pink Etowah marble and gray Creole marble mined in Tate, Georgia, and coquina stone from St. Augustine. The 205-foot-tall tower, which sits on the summit of Iron Mountain, was dedicated on February 1, 1929, by President Calvin Coolidge.

On April 5, 1941, the Section invited Miami-based artist Denman Fink to paint a mural for the Lake Wales Post Office (fig. 2.4). A Works Progress Administration project, the standard plan post office was built in 1940 (fig. 2.5) under the authority of federal works administrator John M. Carmody, commissioner of public buildings W. Englebert Reynolds, and supervising architect Louis A. Simon. The one-story brick structure is streamlined in style with Art Deco accents in the light fixtures and glass insets in the front door.

Fink was an established artist when he moved to South Florida in 1925 to plan the new city of Coral Gables. Born in Springdale, Pennsylvania, he attended the Pittsburgh School of Design, the Museum School of Fine

2.3 Old Atlantic Coast Line Railroad Depot, now a museum, Lake Wales, Florida, February 7, 2010. *Photograph by Ebyabe, courtesy of Wikipedia Commons.*

Arts, and the Art Students League of New York. In Florida, he served as the founding art director of the Coral Gables Corporation, where he was responsible for leading the city planning board. In 1927, he joined the faculty of the University of Miami in its School of Architecture and retired as head of the Art Department in 1952. He was a prolific artist and magazine illustrator who exhibited at the National Academy of Design, the City Art Museum of St. Louis, the Corcoran Gallery, and the Art Institute of Chicago. Fink had previously completed a mural for the post office and courthouse in Miami, so the commission was noncompetitive. The Section requested a mural of 14'6"x3'3" for which Fink was paid $1,200.

Fink visited Lake Wales and met with the postmaster before choosing his subject, a landscape of a working citrus farm with Bok Tower in the distance (fig. 2.6). Blending the natural and built environments, the mural, which offers an impressionistic view of the landscape and pays homage to Central Florida's citrus industry, was installed in July 1942 (Plate 20). The postmaster, George W. Oliver, responded positively to its theme, saying, "This painting lends dignity and individuality to our lobby. It will be a great

*LW.16—U. S. Post Office, Lake Wales, Fla.
The Singing Tower at the Extreme Right*

2.4 U.S. Post Office, Lake Wales, Florida, circa 1947. Postcard Collection, Florida Memory Project. *Courtesy of the State Archives of Florida.*

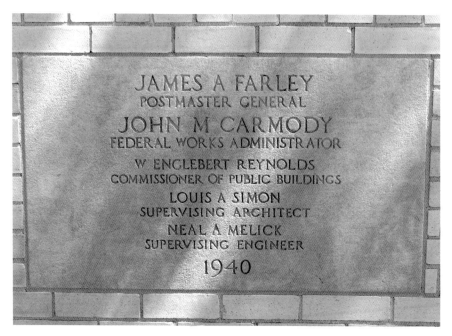

2.5 Lake Wales Post Office cornerstone, Lake Wales, Florida, 2023. *Photograph by Cliff Watson, courtesy of the author.*

2.6 Denman Fink, *Harvest Time–Lake Wales*, 1942. Detail. Lake Wales Post Office, Lake Wales, Florida. *Photograph by Cliff Watson, courtesy of the author.*

source of enjoyment, not only for us, but for the thousands of visitors from all parts of the world, who came to Lake Wales to see the Mountain Lake Singing Tower. It is the only painting of a Public Building in Lake Wales, and we are sure it will be of special interest to the youth of the community and to art students throughout the country."

The mural is dominated by the landscape, which is painted in pale pinks, blues, and greens. The pink granite bell tower punctuates the horizon line, denoting Iron Mountain. In the foreground, Fink has included Black and White laborers working side by side picking, crating, and loading citrus (fig. 2.7). Ladders, trucks, tractor, and crates litter the landscape as dozens of men work to bring in the harvest. Unlike the image of White Crackers sketched by Marjorie Kinnan Rawlings in her Pulitzer Prize–winning novel *The Yearling* (1938) or the caricatured images of African Americans found in George Snow Hill's mural for the Milton Post Office, Fink's painting presents an integrated labor force of realistically depicted individuals. Although Black people in Central Florida were not immune to the horrors of life in the Jim Crow South, there were opportunities

2.7 Denman Fink, *Harvest Time–Lake Wales*, 1942. Detail. Lake Wales Post Office, Lake Wales, Florida. *Photograph by Cliff Watson, courtesy of the author.*

for property ownership and autonomy in the citrus market. Smaller farms could support families, and the 1920 census revealed that 51 percent of Black famers were landowners. Although some White Northerners, like Edward Bok and Marjorie Kinnan Rawlings, came to Florida seeking winter vacation homes, White and Black southerners came to Florida for better economic opportunities, and African Americans moving to Florida found the small independent farms promoted by Central Florida's boosters provided a degree of economic freedom denied them in other southern states. In Central Florida, many Black farmers created independent groves or held wage-earning positions as farm laborers that offered year-round employment. Although packinghouses were staffed primarily with White women, land managers preferred to hire Black men to harvest citrus, a fact reflected in Fink's mural, which captures the energy of the harvest and the diversity of Florida's workforce while celebrating the beauty and fecundity of Lake Wales's agricultural landscape.

HIGHLANDS HAMMOCK STATE PARK

5931 HAMMOCK ROAD
SEBRING, FL 33872

From Lake Wales follow US Highway 27 south thirty miles and you'll find yourself in Sebring, home to both a post office mural and a state park. Highlands Hammock State Park, an ancient subtropical forest on the Lake Wales Ridge, was the first state park in Florida to receive a Civilian Conservation Corps camp in 1933 (fig. 2.8). Acquired in 1929 and developed as a private park through the efforts of the Tropical Florida Parks Association, it opened to the public in 1931 and was transferred to the state in early 1935.

First envisioned as a wildlife sanctuary, the landscape of Highlands Hammock is covered with cypresses, ferns, wild sour orange, avocado, and coffee trees, needle palms, magnolias, wild swamp maples, oaks, and gums. Despite the park's abundant plant and wildlife, the *WPA Guide to Florida* noted, somewhat paradoxically, that "almost every section of the

2.8 Civilian Conservation Corps structure at Highlands Hammock State Park, Sebring, Florida, February 2004. *Photograph by Mwanner, courtesy of Wikipedia Commons.*

2.9 Swamp Trail, Highlands Hammock State Park, Sebring, Florida, February 27, 2011. *Photograph by Ebyabe, courtesy of Wikipedia Commons.*

park is accessible, and improvements have been made to carefully preserve Highlands Hammock as a part of primeval Florida."

Indeed, the area has more rare and endemic species than any other park in the state. Once the habitat of mastodons, saber-toothed tigers, giant ground sloths, and tortoises, the park grounds yielded mastodon tusks and a giant tortoise shell during excavations. In the Pre-Columbian era, the area was inhabited by Jororo people, and there are several mounds located in the park as well. In June 1933, the first of three Civilian Conservation Corps camps was established at the park. Young men employed by the Civilian Conservation Corps planted trees, expanded the original park, and developed the Florida Botanical Garden and Arboretum. Many of the park's structures, including the museum and camp store, picnic pavilions, restrooms, maintenance buildings, greenhouse, sawmill, slat growing houses, and the Herbarium were constructed by young men working for the Civilian Conservation Corps during the 1930s.

With the completion of most of the basic park facilities, Highlands Hammock State Park opened to the public as a state park in August 1935, and in 1941 the Civilian Conservation Corps camp published a brochure that directed visitors to "see the beauty of Florida's unspoiled nature." Many of the park's vistas were created intentionally, however, and as in other state parks, men working for the Civilian Conservation Corps at Highlands Hammock removed native species, imported exotic flowers and shrubs, and moved rivers to craft this "primeval" landscape.

In recognition of the importance of the Civilian Conservation Corps to the Florida Park Service, a museum opened in an original Civilian Conservation Corps building in 1994 (Plate 21). A bronze statue of a Civilian Conservation Corps worker beckons visitors, and docents offer tours where you can learn more about the New Deal and the history of the park through interactive exhibits. Documentary films featuring the oral histories of former Civilian Conservation Corps enrollees can be viewed on the museum stage.

Highlands Hammock State Park boasts more than nine thousand acres of cypress swamps, marshes, pinelands, and scrub and oak hammocks, as well as nine hiking trails. Part of the East Section of the Great Florida Birding and Wildlife Trail, the park provides a diversity of habitat for wading birds, raptors, songbirds, migratory birds, and ducks. Boardwalks (fig. 2.9) over the water and a canal tram tour allow up-close viewing of alligators. This park is a great place to see Florida scrub-jays, crested caracaras, and sandhill cranes.

Charles R. Knight (1874–1953)

Prehistoric Life in Florida, 1942

Sebring Post Office
319 West Center Avenue
Sebring, FL 33870

Just fifteen minutes northeast of Highlands Hammock State Park, you'll find the mural painted for the Sebring Post Office hanging in the Sebring Public Library. Settled in 1912, Sebring lies on the southern end of the Lake Wales Ridge, which formed millions of years ago through the rising and falling of sea levels when most of Florida was underwater. Today it provides a habitat for many rare plants and animals. The highest and oldest ridge in Florida, the Lake Wales Ridge extends one hundred miles from Clermont to Sebring.

2.10 Florida scrub on the Lake Wales Ridge, Lake Wales, Florida, December 18, 2013. *Courtesy of the Forest Service, U.S. Department of Agriculture.*

Part of the Florida Scrub ecosystem (fig. 2.10), one of the most endangered natural plant communities in the United States, it is characterized by the dominance of shrubs. In contrast to forests, which are composed of trees, and savannas and prairies that are largely grasses, the Florida Scrub is a unique plant community that is home to dozens of plant and animal species that occur nowhere else in the world. The white sands of the scrubs along the Lake Wales Ridge are even visible in satellite photographs of Florida taken from space. Sebring's mural (Plate 22) appropriately depicts a natural scene unpopulated by humans. Instead, a saber-toothed tiger family (fig. 2.11) and two woolly mammoths (fig. 2.12) walk amid a moss-draped oak, a few palm trees, and saw palmettos.

The Sebring Post Office mural was painted by Charles R. Knight (fig. 2.13), who was selected for the project without competition. Born in 1874 in Brooklyn, New York, Knight was a well-known painter of dinosaurs and other prehistoric animals, and an illustrator for *National Geographic* magazine. He painted nearly one thousand portraits of animals representing eight hundred different species over the course of his lifetime, and his meticulous recreations, which were based on fossils, were used in natural history museums across the country for years. In 1946, he published *Life Through*

Top: 2.11 Charles R. Knight, *Prehistoric Life in Florida*, 1942. Detail. Originally for the Sebring Post Office, now in the public library, Sebring, Florida. *Photograph by Cliff Watson, courtesy of the author.*

Bottom: 2.12 Charles R. Knight, *Prehistoric Life in Florida*, 1942. Detail. Originally for the Sebring Post Office, now in the public library, Sebring, Florida. *Photograph by Cliff Watson, courtesy of the author.*

2.13 Portrait of
Charles R. Knight
working on a
stegosaurus, 1899.
*Courtesy of Wikipedia
Commons.*

the Ages, a beautifully illustrated look at animals of the prehistoric past.
Although new discoveries and ongoing research have changed the view of
many of the animals Knight depicted, his work remains valuable to both
scientists and artists.

Knight made a trip to Florida to do research, during which he met the
Sebring postmaster and gave a lecture on prehistoric animal life in Florida in
Palm Beach. His mural, for which he was paid $870, was hung in the Sebring
Post Office in March 1942. It was then stored at the new post office from
1985 until 1994, then moved to the Historical Society Archives Building.
Today, you'll find it at the Sebring Library, where it has hung since 2001.

CONCLUSION

Two post offices and two state parks were established in Central Florida
during the Great Depression. The Works Progress Administration
provided funds for the post offices, the Treasury Section of Painting and
Sculpture ensured their decoration, and the Civilian Conservation Corps
established parks to preserve and conserve Florida's unique ecosystems,
including pine-filled flatwoods, scrubs, prairies, marshes, rivers, and oak
hammocks. These state parks, post offices, and decorative murals attest
to the diversity of Florida's architecture and ecology, featuring and
highlighting the region's natural ecosystems. Murals created by Charles
R. Knight and Denman Fink appeal to viewers past and present because
of their narrative content, which captures the region's landscapes, both
wild and tamed.

III

SOUTH FLORIDA

South Florida denotes the southernmost part of the continental United States and the lower part of the peninsula from Sarasota down to the Everglades in the west and Fort Pierce to Homestead in the east. Dominated by the Miami metropolitan area, it also contains the Florida Keys, Naples, Fort Myers, and the Treasure Coast.

When Spanish explorers arrived in South Florida in the early sixteenth century, they encountered some twenty thousand Indigenous peoples, whom they categorized into six separate tribes: the Calusa, Mayaimi, Tequesta, Jeaga, Jobe, and Ais. The Calusa Empire encompassed Southwest Florida from Charlotte Harbor to Cape Sable and was ruled from the capitol at Calos—modern-day Mound Key. Calos was home to several thousand people, but by the time the British gained control of the region in 1763, many of the Native peoples had died from warfare, enslavement, or exposure to European diseases. Those who remained migrated to Cuba with the Spanish, but after 1750, other Indigenous peoples from Alabama and Georgia (Mvskoke or Muscogee Creek) moved into the area. In Florida, they became known as the Seminole and Miccosukee Indians. Between 1818 and 1858, three wars were fought between the Seminole People and the U.S Army. When the wars ended, many Native peoples had either been forcibly removed to a reservation in Oklahoma or migrated into the Everglades.

Despite the habitation of South Florida for some twelve thousand years, the landscape of the peninsula did not change significantly until Henry

Flagler extended the railroad from St. Augustine to Key West in 1912, after which the state experienced tremendous growth. While just a few thousand people lived in South Florida at the dawn of the twentieth century, by 1930 there were more than fifty thousand people in the region. During the early decades of the twentieth century, Dade, Broward, and Palm Beach Counties grew at rates of more than 100 percent per decade. In recognition of the need to protect the area from overdevelopment, in 1915, the first public land, Royal Palm State Park in Paradise Key, was set aside for preservation and recreation. Royal Palm State Park became the first state park and site of the first Civilian Conservation Corps camp in Florida. In 1925, the Florida legislature passed a law creating the Florida State Park System to "provide public recreation, preserve the natural beauty of the state, and conserve historical buildings" and built Myakka River State Park, which opened to the public in 1942. In 1935, the Public Works Administration began operating in Miami as well and built the Miami Beach Post Office, the Miami Shores Golf Club, and the Coral Gables Fire Station. Finally, the Treasury Section of Painting and Sculpture commissioned twelve murals and three sculptures for post offices and federal buildings in South Florida. A thirteenth mural commissioned by the Public Buildings Administration decorates the post office in Lake Worth.

Myakka River State Park

13208 State Rd 72
Sarasota, FL 34241

Just twenty miles east of Sarasota, you'll find Myakka River State Park (Plate 23). Developed from 1934 to 1941 by young men working on the Civilian Conservation Corps, Myakka offers visitors the opportunity to experience a natural subtropical river floodplain. Much of Myakka was bought in 1934 from A.B. Edwards, an executive with the Phoenix Insurance Company. Under the supervision of superintendent Claude Ragan, the Civilian Conservation Corps built shelters, paved the park drive, and erected fences, a contact station, restrooms, and an amphitheater at the park. They also built five rental cabins out of sabal palm logs. The park opened to the public on February 28, 1941, and many of the buildings constructed on its grounds by the Civilian Conservation Corps are still in use today.

3.1 Twenty-five feet above ground in the canopy of an oak and pine forest, Myakka River State Park, June 14, 2019. *Photograph by Troy Jacobson, courtesy of Wikipedia Commons.*

Rather than simply preserving or conserving natural resources, the Civilian Conservation Corps altered the environment of South Florida to suit the needs of recreation and tourism. Like the directors of the National Park Service and the Florida Parks Service, the Civilian Conservation Corps leaders believed that nature was a wild entity that needed to be tamed and beautified. Indeed mosquitoes, alligators, and rattlesnakes were consistent issues at Myakka, where outbreaks of malaria were common among Civilian Conservation Corps enrollees. The Myakka River was prone to flooding, the prairie offered no shade, and the water produced from a well on the property was not potable. Parks were considered nature "improved upon by human labor," or, as the Civilian Conservation Corps superintendent for Myakka River State Park wrote in 1935, "It seems to have always been the rule for men to pick up where nature left off and complete a beautification project."

Although the Civilian Conservation Corps adapted the natural landscape to conform to 1930s-era conceptions of what a public park should look like, Myakka remains a vital part of the southeastern conifer forests ecoregion, offering a mixture of pine forests dominated by longleaf pines, oak hammocks, scrubby flatwoods, dry prairies, marshy and forested wetlands, and bald cypress domes. The dry prairie, comprising grasses and saw palmetto, is of particular importance at Myakka River State Park. Compared in brochures issued by the Civilian Conservation Corps and Florida Park Service to the "African veldt," the dry prairie is the second-most biodiverse ecosystem in North America and unique to Florida. There are just three dry prairies in the state, all of which are located in South Florida near Lake Okeechobee. Dry prairies provide a habitat for several rare species, including Florida burrowing owls, crested caracaras,

3.2 Wildflowers at Myakka River State Park, n.d. *Courtesy of the Florida Park Service.*

grasshopper sparrows, and Florida panthers. Additionally, the Myakka is the only river in the state designated by the legislature as a Wild and Scenic River, meaning it is protected and preserved by congressional order.

Today, Myakka River State Park conserves over thirty-seven thousand acres and is part of a larger area of eighty thousand acres referred to as "Myakka Island." A 135-foot-deep sinkhole appropriately named Deep Hole is located on the northwest bank of the Myakka River, and the park is a great place to observe wildlife. Myakka features miles of hiking trails, including the famed Canopy Walk (fig. 3.1) built by the Civilian Conservation Corps. You can also rent kayaks and canoes for traveling down the river. If you are interested in boating, summer is the best time to visit, as the river can dry up in spring, but this dramatic shift in water levels provides diverse, seasonal visitor experiences. Visit the park's Big Flats Marsh in mid-May to see the Coreopsis, the official state wildflower, in full bloom as rolling fields of yellow flowers cover the ground (fig. 3.2).

Constance Ortmayer (1902–1988)

Arcadia, 1939

Arcadia Post Office
109 North Polk Street
Arcadia, FL 34266

Just thirty miles west of Myakka is the town of Arcadia. Founded in the late nineteenth century when the railroad was built through its center, Arcadia was known for its cattle and citrus. First called Waldron's Landing, then Raulerson's Landing and Tater Hill Bluff, and finally Arcadia, the town built its first post office in 1883 and was named the seat of DeSoto County in 1888. Incorporated as a town in 1886, Arcadia reincorporated as a city in 1901, as it prospered with the building of three railroads, the western route of the Dixie Highway, a tourist camp, and the All-Florida Chautauqua Amphitheatre. Today the DeSoto County Historical Society lists twenty-four buildings on its walking tour of historical buildings, including the post office (fig. 3.3). Built by the Works Progress Administration in 1937 under the supervision of architect Louis A. Simon, it follows the standard rectangular floor plan. It is the only structure in Arcadia built in the Art

3.3 Historical postcard of the Arcadia Post Office, 1944. Postcard Collection, Florida Memory Project. *Courtesy of the State Archives of Florida.*

Moderne style, and it is distinguished by its sleek, horizontal design and minimal ornamentation.

Rather than a painting, the Arcadia Post Office is decorated with a charming plaster relief sculpture (fig. 3.4) of Florida's agricultural history. Depicting two men, two women, and a young boy with a cow and its calf pictured under an arch of orange trees, the relief is a pastoral, or an idealized scene of the shepherd lifestyle. This genre usually shows men herding livestock or celebrates agriculture, and in this case, the man at the left picks oranges and hands them to the woman who collects them in her apron. A shirtless young man behind a cow holds a bushel basket full of some sort of gourd on his shoulder. A young boy sits before the cow and its calf, perhaps milking it, as a young woman pets the cow and holds a pail of milk. The image evokes a familial group, perhaps three generations working together on a family farm.

Like the relief sculptures made for the 1939 New York World's Fair, *Arcadia* is made of plaster painted white and follows the conventions of the then popular archaic or Greco Deco style, one that blends the linear precision and stiffness of ancient Greek art with the smooth contours of Art Deco and one appropriate for placement in Arcadia's Art Moderne post office. During the 1930s and 1940s, the National Sculpture Society promoted

3.4 Constance Ortmayer, *Arcadia*, 1939. Plaster. Arcadia Post Office, Arcadia, Florida. *Courtesy of the National Archives and Records Administration.*

realistic, figurative sculpture, and this work followed that trend. The relief was sculpted by Constance Ortmayer, who after studying at Bryn Mawr and the Royal Academy of Fine Arts in Vienna, was selected to serve as the technical advisor for sculpture for the Section of Fine Arts. She was awarded the commission in Arcadia based on her work for the Section, and after completing the Arcadia Post Office relief, she was invited to join the faculty of Rollins College in Winter Park, where she taught until 1968. In addition to her sculpture for the post office in Arcadia, she also completed *Alabama Agriculture* (1940) for the post office in Scottsboro, Alabama, the following year. The pieces are similar in style and composition, though they diverge in the industries depicted. Ortmayer said of the Scottsboro piece,

Three phases of cotton growing form the theme of the central panel. On the right the cultivation of the crop is symbolized by the young man working with a hoe among the new plants. Opposite a young woman is depicted picking ripened bolls, and for the background, the processing and shipping

of cotton is represented by the bales and the strong figure of a second young worker standing between them. Both of the flanking panels interpret the growing of corn. The young man and woman shown on the right are examining the fruit on the ripened stalks and the couple on the left are represented as workers who have harvested the new crop.

The Treasury Section of Fine Arts, which commissioned the piece, wrote of the work, "In a sculpture characterized by clean, flowing lines, Miss Ortmayer gives an exceptionally effective representation of the youthful strength and grace that each new generation brings to the agriculture of the South." The same can be said of the Arcadia relief, which shows three generations working in Central Florida in its two most important industries: citrus and cattle.

LUCILE BLANCH (1895–1981)

Osceola Holding Informal Court with His Chiefs, 1938

FORT PIERCE POST OFFICE
315 AVENUE A
FORT PIERCE, FL 34954

Head east out of Arcadia on Highway 70 for one hundred miles and you'll reach Fort Pierce. One of the oldest communities along Florida's east coast, Fort Pierce was named for an army installation built there during the Second Seminole War. Following the war, Fort Pierce's accessible waterways and Henry Flagler's railroad made the city an important transportation center.

On October 10, 1938, the Section invited Lucile Blanch (fig. 3.5) to submit designs for the Fort Pierce Post Office. A well-known and respected artist, Blanch was born in Hawley, Minnesota, in 1895 and studied painting and printmaking at the Minneapolis School of Art. She then attended the Art Students League of New York, where she studied under Kenneth Hayes Miller, the leader of the Fourteenth Street School of artists known for their social realist style. Around 1930, Lucile Blanch and her husband, Arnold Blanch, lived in San Francisco, where they became close friends with Frida Kahlo and her husband, the Mexican muralist Diego Rivera.

3.5 Portrait of
Lucile Blanch,
1930. Black-and-
white photograph,
8" x 10". Peter
A. Juley & Son
Collection, Archives
of American Art.
*Courtesy of Wikipedia
Commons.*

She also was a co-founder of the Woodstock Art Colony and received a Guggenheim Fellowship in 1933. She taught at the Ringling School of Art in Sarasota, Florida, from 1935 to 1936.

Blanch came to the attention of the Section in 1934 when she was included in an exhibition reviewed by Forbes Watson, an art critic and the chief advisor of the Section. Drawing on the Indigenous history of Fort Pierce and its role in the Seminole Wars, Blanch submitted two preliminary sketches to the Washington office, both of which included images of the Seminole leader Osceola. Osceola was a celebrity in his own time who fascinated his contemporaries and was the subject of numerous books, plays, poems, and paintings. Born near Tuskegee, Alabama, in 1804, Osceola was raised by his Muscogee mother. His youth in Alabama was tumultuous, as White settler colonists pressured the federal government to remove the Native population from the new territory. This resulted in the Creek Wars, after which Osceola, along with other refugees who had resisted assimilation and fought White encroachment, migrated to Florida to join the newly emerging Seminole tribe. In 1818, he and his family were captured by Andrew Jackson and then released. As an adult, he was given the name Asi-yahola—*asi*, referring to a ceremonial caffeinated tea made from the native yaupon holly, and *yahola*, meaning to shout or sing— Anglicized as Osceola. This name, loosely translated as Shouting Black Drink or Black Drink Singer, offers a hint to Osceola's dynamic personality.

Blanch's mural (Plate 24) for the Fort Pierce post office presents viewers with a detailed, colorful, and charming rendering of Osceola, along with other Seminole men, women, and children amid palm trees and oak hammocks. An idyllic, yet industrious, view of early Florida life, the mural shows Chief Osceola standing in conversation with three men, while a younger man stands above a recently slain Florida panther and another man fishes along the Indian River. Two women in colorful Seminole patchwork dresses stand beneath a chickee hut with a young boy. As the Seminole people went into hiding after the Second Seminole War, they were joined by Americans of African descent who had escaped bondage on southern plantations. Within this environment, the art of Seminole patchwork was born. Unlike quilts made by enslaved people of African descent, Seminole patchwork is characterized by the strategic tearing and placement of strips of new, rather than recycled, cloth. In addition to manufactured textiles and

3.6 Exterior of the Old City Hall, Fort Pierce, Florida, September 27, 2009. *Photograph by Sebas Torrente, courtesy of Wikipedia Commons.*

synthetic dyes, sewing machines were introduced to Seminole communities in the early 1900s and played an important role in the development of the art form. Colorful strips were sewn together, edge-to-edge, to form a variety of geometric patterns for shirts, jackets, and skirts. Blanch includes Seminole patchwork in the mural, which she completed with palm trees and oak hammocks to connote a tropical landscape. Unable to visit Florida due to teaching commitments, Blanch obviously consulted George Catlin's famous portrait of Osceola, as well as Thomas McKenney and James Hall's *History of the Indian Tribes of North America* (1838), from which she borrowed the design and colors of Osceola's clothing.

In addition to the mural for Fort Pierce, Blanch painted *Appalachia* for the Appalachia, Virginia post office; *Crossing the Battle of Blue Licks* for the Flemingsburg, Kentucky Post Office (1943); and *Rural Mississippi—From Early Days to Present* for the post office in Tylertown, Mississippi (1941). The latter is among the murals that have been recently covered by the U.S. Postal Service.

Today Blanch's mural of Osceola hangs in the Old City Hall (fig. 3.6), a historic Mediterranean Revival and Italian Renaissance Revival–style building in downtown Fort Pierce. It was designed by architect William Hatcher and built by C.E. Cahow in 1925 at the peak of the Florida land boom.

CHARLES ROSEN (1878–1950)

Landscape and Seminole Indians, 1938

OLD PALM BEACH POST OFFICE
95 NORTH COUNTY ROAD
PALM BEACH, FL 33480

Travel sixty-five miles south of Fort Pierce to reach the Palm Beach Post Office. Settlers who moved to Palm Beach County in the nineteenth century lived around the twenty-two-mile-long Lake Worth, named after Colonel William Jenkins Worth, who helped end the Second Seminole War in 1842. People made their homes on Hypoluxo Island, near the south end of the lake, and on Palm Beach, on the east side of the lake. Although the Palm Beach homesteads stretched from the lake to the ocean, most settlers built on

3.7 Exterior of the Palm Beach Post Office from Royal Poinciana Way, Palm Beach, Florida, 2008. *Photograph by Christopher Ziemnowicz, courtesy of Wikipedia Commons.*

the lake rather than the ocean side of the island. The middle of the island, and their property, was swampland, plagued by alligators and mosquitoes. By the 1930s, most of the island was drained, and in 1936 the Works Progress Administration constructed a post office in the middle of the island at the end of Royal Poinciana Way (fig. 3.7). A striking example of the Spanish Colonial Revival style, it features a ceramic tile roof and a beautiful wood beam ceiling with inlay accents.

To complete the building's decoration, the Section invited Charles Rosen to submit designs on a noncompetitive basis. Rosen had studied under William Merritt Chase and Frank DuMond at the National Academy of Design and New York School of Art and was the recipient of numerous awards. A landscape painter, printmaker, and teacher, he was a leader of the Woodstock Art Colony and an associate member of the National Academy of Design. In addition to the murals for the Palm Beach Post Office, Rosen was commissioned to paint murals for post offices in Beacon and Poughkeepsie, New York. Rosen planned a trip to Palm Beach to experience the area firsthand and find inspiration for his composition.

3.8 Charles Rosen, landscape, 1938. Oil on canvas, 5' x 7'4". Left and right panels. Palm Beach Post Office, Palm Beach, Florida. *Photograph by Cliff Watson, courtesy of the author.*

Rosen's first design depicted Flagler's railroad flanked by his hotels, the Breakers and La Poinciana. The Section rejected the sketch, requesting a scene of Native American life instead.

In response, Rosen visited a Seminole tourist village. The decline in the hide trade and the Great Depression had forced the Seminole people to find alternative sources of income, such as selling handicrafts, including patchwork clothing and dolls, to tourists. Although they had been making dolls as toys for their children for years, with the rise of tourism, doll making became big business. Colorful patchwork patterns attracted travelers, and as demand grew, baskets, beadwork, woodworking, and dolls were adapted to satisfy consumer tastes and interests.

After his visit to the tourist village, Rosen reworked his mural design to the delight of the Washington office. The finished mural is in three parts. The left and right panels (fig. 3.8) depict palm trees along the lake and beach. The center panel (Plate 25) offers vignettes of Seminole life as observed in the tourist village. On the left, a man in a canoe gathers sawgrass from a marsh. On the right, two men dress a recently hunted wild turkey. In the center, two men are shaded by a chickee hut while women are shown making dolls with the palmetto fibers harvested in the marsh. Techniques were traditionally passed down from mother to daughter or shared within the matrilineal community, as depicted in Rosen's mural. Rosen has paid special attention to the patchwork dress of the Seminole people, a detail which was praised in the local press for its "beauty and appropriateness." Rosen was paid $1,650 for the mural, which was completed in May 1938.

Stevan Dohanos (1907–1994)

Legend of James Edward Hamilton, Barefoot Mailman, 1939–41

West Palm Beach Post Office
3200 Summit Boulevard
West Palm Beach, FL 33406

Travel back across the Lake Worth Lagoon from the Old Post Office in Palm Beach to the mainland and head six miles south to find Stevan Dohanos's *Legend of James Edward Hamilton, Barefoot Mailman*, one of the most popular post office murals in the state. Created for the West Palm Beach Post Office on South Olive Avenue in 1940, Dohanos's six murals, for which he received $2,400, feature James Edward "Ed" Hamilton, "Florida's Barefoot Mail Carrier." The subject is historical, referring to the men who worked the Barefoot Mail Route established between Jupiter and Miami in 1885 to facilitate mail service. In conducting his research for the murals, Dohanos visited West Palm Beach and corresponded with Charles W. Pierce, the postmaster in Boynton Beach, who had worked the Barefoot Route and served as the model for the mailman in the murals. Prior to the introduction of this 136-mile route—56 miles over water and the other 80 over sand—mail made the 3,000-mile journey from Jupiter, Florida, up to New York City and back down through Havana, Cuba, by ship before arriving up to six weeks later in Miami. Working the Barefoot Mail Route was a strenuous, dangerous, and heroic job. Florida was largely unsettled at this time, and the route was plagued by alligators. The barefoot mail carrier risked his life to help people get their mail in a timely fashion, all for an annual salary of $600, the equivalent of about $13,000 today.

The most famous Barefoot Mailman was James Edward "Ed" Hamilton, who was killed at Hillsboro Inlet in October 1887. Described in Pierce's memoir *Pioneer Life in Southeast Florida* as "only thirty-three at the time, strong and active, six feet tall in his stocking feet and weighing one hundred and eighty pounds; he was an excellent swimmer and well able to take care of himself on land or in the water." It is believed that he tried to swim across the inlet after discovering that someone had taken his boat. His body was never found, but his mail satchel and clothes were found on the beach. Some speculate that he was killed by alligators, sharks, or a barracuda, but others believe it was murder. Hamilton's story was so compelling that Theodore Pratt wrote *The Barefoot Mailman* (1943), a novel inspired by life, which was adapted into a film starring Robert Cummings (released in 1951). The barefoot route was discontinued in 1892 when the rock road from Jupiter to Miami was completed. Henry John Burkhardt was the last of the barefoot mailmen.

Dohanos, who was born in 1907 in Lorain, Ohio, was relatively unknown when he was hired to paint the West Palm Beach Post Office, but he would go on to become the second-most prolific illustrator (after Norman Rockwell) of the *Saturday Evening Post*. His first cover appeared on March 7, 1942, and over the course of the next fifteen years, he produced more than one hundred covers. Dohanos's work has been compared to that of Edward Hopper, but he described himself as "a spiritual child of the Ash Can School," saying, "Almost any subject when treated with care and respect can relate to the human condition in a meaningful and poignant way." Certainly, this is the case with his murals created for the West Palm Beach Post Office, which, after being on public display for forty-four years at the Olive Avenue office, were removed from the walls, restored, and rehung in 1984 at the new distribution center on Summit Avenue. They remain there to this day, accessible to audiences during business hours. Three of the studies for the West Palm Beach Post Office murals are in the collection of the Smithsonian American Art Museum and have been displayed at the Library of Congress (figs. 3.9–3.11).

3.9 Stevan Dohanos, Panel 2, *Legend of James Edward Hamilton—Barefoot Mailman* (mural study, West Palm Beach, Florida Post Office), 1940, watercolor on paperboard, sheet: 14⅛" x 22" (35.9 x 56.0 cm). *Smithsonian American Art Museum, Transfer from the General Services Administration, 1982.20.1.*

Top: 3.10 Stevan Dohanos, Panel 5, *Legend of James Edward Hamilton—Barefoot Mailman* (mural study, West Palm Beach, Florida Post Office), 1940, watercolor on paperboard, sheet: 14" x 22" (35.6 x 55.9 cm). *Smithsonian American Art Museum, Transfer from the General Services Administration, 1982.20.2.*

Bottom: 3.11 Stevan Dohanos, Panel 6, *Legend of James Edward Hamilton—Barefoot Mailman* (mural study, West Palm Beach, Florida Post Office), 1940, watercolor on paperboard, sheet: 14⅛" x 22" (35.9 x 55.9 cm). *Smithsonian American Art Museum, Transfer from the General Services Administration, 1982.20.3.*

The first panel (fig. 3.12) depicts the barefoot mailman embarking on his route from the Jupiter Lighthouse. The 105-foot-tall lighthouse, which was completed in 1860, sits at the junction of the Indian River and the Jupiter Inlet. In the background, the lighthouse keeper and his wife are pictured standing to the left of the doorway and behind a pile of split logs. The lighthouse keeper holds an axe, and his wife holds the hem of her apron

3.12 Stevan Dohanos, *Legend of James Edward Hamilton, Mail Carrier*, 1939. Oil on canvas, 8' x 4' West Palm Beach Post Office, West Palm Beach, Florida. *Photograph by Cliff Watson, courtesy of the author.*

up to her waist. The inclusion of the axe alludes to the self-reliance of Florida pioneers and the dangers of life on the frontier. In the upper right-hand corner, two pelicans fly through the early morning gray sky above a cypress tree. The position of the birds, the cypress, and the couple directs the viewers' attention to Hamilton, who occupies the center-left foreground of the painting. Three palm trees and long grasses sway in the strong sea breeze behind him. Dohanos has created a stylized version of the trees, not unlike those created by Grant Wood in his views of the Midwest. The elements of the painting, including the overcast sky and the determined look on Hamilton's face, work together to foreshadow the tragedy of Hamilton's disappearance on October 10, 1887.

In the second panel (Plate 26), Hamilton accepts the mail from the postmaster before starting his six-day round trip to Miami. Postmasters in rural Florida worked from their homes, and here the canceling of the registered mail is completed on a table set up on the front porch. The atmosphere is both tropical and domestic, with large aloe and ponytail and fan palms surrounding the men.

The third panel (Plate 27) shows the barefoot mailman accompanied by two travelers. Mailmen sometimes escorted people down to Miami, and their inclusion shows one of the many ways that postal workers, and by extension the federal government, helped the local community. Dohanos has depicted Hamilton in his characteristic bare feet with his pants rolled up above his knees, whereas his guests are in full dress suits, hats, and shoes. The

3.13 Stevan Dohanos, *Legend of James Edward Hamilton, Mail Carrier*, 1939. Oil on canvas, 8' x 4'. West Palm Beach Post Office, West Palm Beach, Florida. *Photograph by Cliff Watson, courtesy of the author.*

middle-aged man in the center wears a dark suit and bowler hat, while the older man wears a light-colored suit and straw hat. By varying their age and costume, Dohanos alludes to the variety of people who lived and worked in Florida at the time. A large piece of driftwood fills half the composition, but the figures are larger than life and pushed to the foreground.

The fourth painting (Plate 28) depicts Hamilton striding through the sand next to the prow and figurehead of a shipwreck as two great blue herons rest on the wreckage. The inclusion of the prow attests to the numerous shipwrecks that washed up on Florida's shores in the late nineteenth century. Some pioneers even reported that they built whole houses out of wood they found on the beach. This is perhaps the most famous of the panels, as it was used as the cover for Pratt's novel.

The fifth painting (Plate 29) shows Hamilton rowing his skiff through a mangrove swamp as three alligators sunbathe in the foreground. This is the only one of the six murals where Hamilton is pictured in the background, a compositional choice that foreshadows the mail carrier's disappearance. The final painting (fig. 3.13) depicts Hamilton pausing on a beach for a drink of coconut milk. Two pelicans, symbols of the crucifixion, rest at his feet next to a blooming yucca. With its pink-hued sky, setting sun, and emblems of sacrifice, the painting creates an appropriate ending to Hamilton's journey and the mural cycle.

The Legend of James Edward Hamilton, Barefoot Mailman was immediately popular and served to reinforce both the significance of a local hero and the perseverance of Florida's pioneers. The panels highlight the various ecosystems of South Florida, including coastal dunes and mangrove swamps, and merges the natural and built environments to create a historical scene that celebrates one of the federal government's most important agencies, the postal service.

Joseph D. Myers (1913–1989)

Settler Fighting Alligator from Rowboat, 1946

Lake Worth Post Office
720 Lucerne Avenue
Lake Worth, FL 33460

Six miles southeast of the West Palm Beach Post Office, you'll find the Lake Worth Post Office on Lucerne Avenue (fig. 3.14). As the population of South Florida grew, new municipalities were created. Samuel and Fannie James, a formerly enslaved couple, were the first non-Native settlers in the area, filing a homestead claim on 187 acres in 1885. Fannie James operated the Jewell Post Office, which served residents who lived between Lantana and West Palm Beach, until 1903. In 1896, Flagler extended his rail line south from West Palm Beach, making the area more accessible to settlers, and Lake Worth was incorporated in 1913 to serve the needs of a land development scheme hatched by the Palm Beach Farms Company that gave a twenty-five-foot lot in the proposed town to anyone who bought five acres of farmland. As a result, Lake Worth grew rapidly during the 1910s and 1920s.

The post office on Lucerne Avenue was constructed in 1930 under the auspices of supervising architect Louis A. Simon and commissioner of public buildings W. Englebert Reynolds. The standard plan is adorned with elements of the Spanish Revival style, including a creamy stucco exterior, terra-cotta barrel tiled hip roof, engaged fluted pilasters framing the doors and windows, and copper awning. The Section commissioned Florida local and Tampa artist Joseph D. Myers to paint a mural to decorate the new post office. He was selected in an anonymous contest by a jury that included architecture faculty at the University of Florida and two Florida artists. Myers's mural (Plate 30) presents viewers with a hunting scene painted in

United States Post Office, Lake Worth, Florida

3.14 Historical postcard of the Lake Worth Post Office, circa 1930–45. The Tichnor Brothers Collection. *Courtesy of the Boston Public Library.*

warm earth tones. Two White men and a dog balance in their boat while wrangling an alligator. The standing man ropes the alligator's neck while the seated man holds a rifle on its body. The alligator's open mouth faces off against the dog's snarl, while seabirds circle overhead. The composition is dynamic with all the figures positioned diagonally. The waves created by the central activity radiate out in concentric circles drawing attention to the dramatic showdown between settlers and untamed nature.

The Section and the artist "squabbled for months over the design, with the administrator calling a revised sketch 'disappointing' and complaining that among other things, 'the dog is in no way convincing.'" Installation was delayed until 1947 due to issues with the building, but Myers was eventually paid the $1,000 he was promised for the work. Although the painting is among the most exciting of Florida's post office murals, it has received mixed reviews. As Mark Berger, manager of the Lake Worth Post Office, said in 2015, "It is a little dark, to say the least."

DENMAN FINK (1880–1956)

Law Guides Florida Progress, 1940

ALEXANDER SAMBUGNAC (1888–1965)

Love and Hope, 1938
Wisdom and Courage, 1938

DAVID W. DYER FEDERAL BUILDING AND UNITED STATES COURTHOUSE
300 NORTHEAST FIRST AVENUE
MIAMI, FL 33132

Head south from Lake Worth about sixty miles, and you'll find the David W. Dyer Federal Building and U.S. Courthouse (fig. 3.15), which originally housed the post office and is home to two stone relief sculptures and a monumental mural funded by the Treasury Section of Painting and Sculpture. After a devastating hurricane decimated South Florida in 1926, Congress appropriated more than $2 million to build a new courthouse in Miami. The Office of the Supervising Architect of the Treasury selected Phineas Paist and Harold D. Steward to design the building, which blends elements of the Renaissance Revival style with Mediterranean embellishments. The façade has a projecting central bay dominated by a colonnade of engaged Corinthian columns. The casement window frames are embossed with chevrons, and the spandrels depict scenes from Florida's history. The interior is elegantly

3.15 U.S. Post Office, Court House and Custom House, 1933. Architects Phineas E. Paist and Harold D. Steward. Renamed the David W. Dyer Federal Building and United States Courthouse in 1997. *Courtesy of the National Archives.*

appointed with eleven different types of marble. A multicolored marble star decorates the center of the lobby's floor. The building is constructed of concrete and steel to withstand hurricane-force winds and is clad in keystone, a lithified coral quarried near Key Largo. Construction began in 1931, and the building opened to the public on July 1, 1933.

When the courthouse opened, it housed all of Miami's federal agencies, including the postal service. The competition for the building's decoration was the first announced in the state. In 1935, even before the Treasury Section of Painting and Sculpture was established, Paist and Steward approved a sketch by Florida artist Denman Fink for a monumental mural to decorate the building. Fink was offered $6,000 to complete the project, but when the Section took over the decoration of federal buildings in October 1934, it established a pay scale based on square footage that not only reduced Fink's stipend to a mere $800 but also required him to reapply for the commission. The Section opened the competition to any artist in the Southeast, and sixty artists submitted designs. Twelve artists, including Fink, were selected as finalists, but the Washington office offered the contract to New York–based artist Charles Chapman. After a letter-writing campaign led by Miami citizens, the Section reopened the competition and Fink's sketch was selected. The mural was not hung in the post office but in a courtroom (fig. 3.16) and appropriately features a scene of justice. The District Courtroom is a large, open, two-story space

3.16 Installation view of Denman Fink's *Law Guides Florida Progress* at the David W. Dyer Federal Building and Courthouse, Miami, Florida, 2007. Carol M. Highsmith Archive, Washington, D.C. *Courtesy of the Library of Congress Prints and Photographs Division.*

that features a beautifully carved wooden bench, jury box, witness stand, and desk. Engaged marble columns frame Fink's 25'3"x11'2" mural, which hangs just above the judge's bench.

Perhaps the most modern of Florida's murals, *Law Guides Florida Progress* (Plate 31) is a colorful and crowded collage-like scene that emphasizes the natural fecundity of the state and the industry of its citizens. Reading the painting from right to left, the viewer finds a scene filled with cypress trees, great blue herons, Native Americans, thatched roof structures, and sailing vessels. In the center, a judge comforts a woman as she holds a baby and stands next to a man with a bandaged head. Behind them an elderly woman cries, while in the foreground—in a scene foreshadowing Fink's mural for Lake Wales—men pack oranges, pineapples, and bananas and weigh fish in a crowded vignette of agricultural industry. To the left, men and women are engaged in the arts and sciences. Fink included likenesses of himself and Paist, with whom he worked in Coral Gables. Fink is represented as the draftsman and Paist the chemist. The mural appears to present an evolutionary history of industry in Florida from hunting and gathering and agriculture to science and tourism.

In addition to Fink's mural, Alexander Sambugnac was commissioned to create two relief sculptures for the courthouse. Born in Zemun, Yugoslavia, in 1888, Sambugnac studied at the Royal Academies of Fine Arts in

3.17 Alexander Sambugnac, *Love and Hope*, 1938. Cast stone, 48"x 72"x 3". David W. Dyer Federal Building and Courthouse, Miami, Florida. New Deal Art Program, Fine Arts Collection. *Courtesy of the U.S. General Services Administration.*

3.18 Alexander Sambugnac, *Wisdom and Courage*, 1938. 36"x72"x3". David W. Dyer Federal Building and Courthouse, Miami, Florida. New Deal Art Program, Fine Arts Collection. *Courtesy of the U.S. General Services Administration.*

Budapest and Munich before going to Paris in 1913 to apprentice under Antoine Bourdelle. Sambugnac became a naturalized U.S. citizen in 1938 and completed sculptures for numerous post offices around the country, including *Communication* for the post office in Rochester, New York. His sculpture *Love and Hope* (fig. 3.17) for the Miami Courthouse shows a young woman playing the lyre, whereas *Wisdom and Courage* (fig. 3.18) depicts a seated male figure gazing at a tablet. These sculptures are unusual for New Deal art, as the two cast-stone lunettes portray nude allegorical figures rather than naturalistic historical scenes.

Charles Russell Hardman (1912–1995)

Themes from Florida History, 1940

Miami Beach Post Office
1300 Washington Avenue
Miami Beach, FL 33119

Venture across Biscayne Bay to Miami Beach where in 1870 Henry Lum and his son Charles arrived by sailboat. In 1913, the first bridge from Miami to

Miami Beach was built and in 1915 Miami Beach was incorporated. Miami Beach witnessed tremendous growth in the 1920s as real estate tycoons from the Northeast built numerous small hotels along lower Collins Avenue and Ocean Drive. Today Miami Beach is famous for this Art Deco District known as South Beach.

The Miami Beach Post Office (fig. 3.19) was commissioned by the Works Progress Administration in 1937. Like the post office in Arcadia, it is built in the Art Moderne or Streamlined Moderne style, a design characterized by its curving forms, long horizontal lines, rounded corners, flat roof, horizontal band of windows, and smooth walls with no ornamentation. Unlike the post office in Arcadia, however, it was not designed by Louis A. Simon but by Howard Lovewell Cheney, who also designed the Federal Building and the Court of Peace at the 1939 New York World's Fair. Cheney's design incorporates a tall circular lobby accented by a fountain, a conical roof, and a tall thin cupola. The main entrance's double doors are topped by a stone eagle and a ten-foot-high wall of glass blocks.

In August 1938, the Section invited Georgia artist Charles Russell Hardman to paint a mural for the lobby's rounded wall (fig. 3.20). Although he was an inexperienced artist with only six months of formal training when he was awarded the $3,000 commission, Hadman had impressed the Section

3.19 Exterior of the Miami Beach Post Office, Miami Beach, Florida, October 20, 2006. *Photograph by Daniel Di Palma, courtesy of Wikipedia Commons.*

Above: 3.20 Charles Russell Hardman, *Episodes from the History of Florida*, 1940. Oil on canvas, Miami Beach Post Office, Miami Beach, Florida. *Photograph by Daniel Di Palma, courtesy of Wikipedia Commons.*

Left: 3.21 Charles Russell Hardman, *Episodes from the History of Florida*, 1940. Miami Beach, Florida, October 20, 2006. *Photograph by Daniel Di Palma, courtesy of Wikipedia Commons.*

with designs he had submitted to a previous competition. Hardman went to Miami Beach and visited the postmaster and members of the Chamber of Commerce who helped him decide on a theme for the mural. His initial sketches depicted the trucking, sugar cane, golf, and citrus industries, but under the direction of the national office, he changed the subject of the mural to the "Discovery of Florida."

In three panels, Hardman conjures scenes from Florida's history beginning on the left (fig. 3.21) with Ponce de León meeting with the Native Calusa people. The long center panel (fig. 3.22) shows Hernando de Soto fighting the Apalachee people. The final panel (fig. 3.23) features U.S. general Thomas Jesup negotiating with the Seminole Nation after the Second Seminole War. Although none of these scenes is particular to Miami, the cycle was well received at its unveiling on January 14, 1941. It was covered by the *Miami Herald*, and the postmaster wrote a letter to the national office praising the work:

Above: 3.22 Charles Russell Hardman, *Episodes from the History of Florida*, 1940, Miami Beach, Florida, October 20, 2006. *Photograph by Daniel Di Palma, courtesy of Wikipedia Commons.*

Left: 3.23 Charles Russell Hardman, *Episodes from the History of Florida*, 1940, Miami Beach, Florida, October 20, 2006. *Photograph by Daniel Di Palma, courtesy of Wikipedia Commons.*

Since its installation it has attracted a great deal of attention and seemingly all favorable....It is a most virile piece of work throughout, and in full harmony with the color tone and architecture of the lobby, and in all, a highly striking artistic job, this, my own opinion seems to be the general opinion of those qualified to judge....I am very proud, personally, of the installation of this Hardman mural, and I feel that the Treasury Art Projects has made an outstanding art acquisition for greater Miami in this work.

Hardman was subsequently awarded a commission for a post office mural in Guntersville, Alabama.

ROYAL PALM STATE PARK

EVERGLADES NATIONAL PARK
PARADISE KEY, FL

Drive fifty-five miles southwest of Miami to find Paradise Key and Royal State Park (so named because it has the largest stand of royal palms in the country). First noted in an 1847 federal land survey, Paradise Key is a twelve-mile-long islet—one of the largest Everglades keys—and an area of great biological diversity. Vines, ferns, and wild orchids grow in abundance, and much of Paradise Key's plant life is found nowhere else in the United States. As scientists

3.24 Natural moat partially surrounding Paradise Key, Homestead, Florida, circa 1900. Postcard Collection, Florida Memory Project. *Courtesy of the State Archives of Florida.*

called for the land to be set aside, the Florida Federation of Women's Clubs acquired 960 acres of the key in 1915, which was matched with another 960 acres donated to the state by Mary Lily Kenan Flagler, Henry Flagler's widow. The park was dedicated on November 23, 1916, the first state park in Florida (fig. 3.24). Over 1,000 people attended the opening, with many more visitors following in subsequent years. In 1921, the state added another 2,080 acres, bringing the total acreage of protected land up to 4,000. Despite its name, it was really a private nonprofit run by May Mann Jennings, who worked hard to keep the park open. Finally in 1933, Jennings was able to lure the Civilian Conservation Corps to the park. They established a Civilian Conservation Corps camp in Florida in Royal State Park when Company 262 was transferred from Niagara Falls, New York, at the request of the Florida Federation of Women's Clubs. Once in Royal Palm, the Civilian Conservation Corps constructed trails and other historic structures for tourists and residents to enjoy (Plate 32). Royal Palm State Park features old-growth live oaks and royal palms in the middle of a wet prairie enclosed with ferns, orchids, and other rare and tropical plants. The establishment of Royal Palm State Park began the conservation efforts that would lead to the designation of the Everglades as a National Park in 1947.

CONCLUSION

Seven post offices and two state parks were established in South Florida under the auspices of the New Deal. The Works Progress Administration and Public Buildings Administration provided funds for the federal buildings, the Treasury Section of Painting and Sculpture ensured their decoration, and the Florida Federation of Women's Clubs and Civilian Conservation Corps helped establish Florida's first state park, Royal Palm State Park, as well as Myakka River State Park to preserve and conserve the natural landscape. The legacy of New Deal–era federal patronage lives on in the buildings, murals, and parks built during this exciting period in South Florida's history. Both the Art Moderne and Mediterranean styles were employed in South Florida's architecture, and the murals created by Constance Ortmayer, Lucile Blanch, Charles Rosen, Stevan Dohanos, Joseph D. Myers, Denman Fink, Alexander Sambugnac, and Charles Russell Hardman continue to appeal to viewers today. Finally, Myakka River State Park and Royal Palm State Park offers visitors encounters with a dry prairie, wet prairie, and subtropical wetland, landscapes unique to South Florida.

The Great Depression came early to Florida, with the collapse of the real estate market sending the state into a severe economic downtown by 1926. With the enactment of Franklin Delano Roosevelt's New Deal, federal programs were created that put the nation, and Florida, to work. The Works Progress Administration, Civil Works Administration, Treasury Section of Painting and Sculpture, and Civilian Conservation Corps were especially significant forms of federal patronage that the state leveraged to attract new visitors and residents, increase tourism, and change the perception of Florida in the national imagination.

In the years immediately following the Civil War, Florida became a particularly popular destination for health tourists in search of warm winter air to relieve pulmonary diseases and stress. In the late nineteenth century, Gilded Age vacationers wintered in Florida, either in their second homes or in one of Henry Flagler's grand hotels, but with the development of the state highway system in the late 1910s and early 1920s, Florida began to cater to middle-class tourists. Boosters and promoters replaced a romanticized view of Florida as part of the Old South with a new neutral image that recalled Florida's Spanish colonial past and situated it as more akin to the French Riviera than to landmarks of the antebellum South like Charleston, South Carolina, and Savannah, Georgia. Early tourist attractions exploited Florida's "exotic" image, promoting alligator wrestling, Seminole villages, and fountains of youth, and the state's booth at the 1933 Century of Progress Exhibition in Chicago presented Florida as a "natural paradise" and "tropical playground."

In 1936, Congress passed the Federal Park, Parkway, and Recreational Area Study Act, which asked state planners to evaluate their conservation efforts and inventory properties that could be developed into parks. The study found that "climate, natural recreation, and parks" were Florida's main attractions. Seizing the opportunity to use federal dollars to develop a system of state parks, Florida legislators designated Royal Palm State Park in Paradise Key the site of the first Civilian Conservation Corps camp in the state. The Civilian Conservation Corps would go on to employ nearly fifty thousand men in Florida and with the help of the Works Progress Administration establish the first ten state parks of the Florida Park Service. Thanks to these federal agencies, people can now visit Florida Caverns State Park in Marianna, Torreya State Park in Rock Bluff, O'Leno State Park in High Springs, Mike Roess Gold Head Branch State Park in Keystone Heights, Ravine Gardens State Park in Palatka, Fort Clinch State Park in Fernandina Beach, Hillsborough River State Park in Thonotosassa, Highlands Hammock State Park in Sebring, Myakka River State Park in Sarasota, and Royal Palm State Park in Paradise Key and see the impact of the New Deal in Florida.

State parks both alter and conserve the natural environment, influencing our perception of the Florida landscape, as do representations of the natural and built environment created for the state's post offices. Post office murals are visible and enduring symbols of New Deal ideology that not only provide lasting evidence of governmental art patronage during the Great Depression but also reveal a community's relationship to their environment and history at a particular moment. Among the most frequently visited of federal buildings, post offices have historically operated as community gathering spaces, and their murals are among the most viewed examples of public art. Not just for picking up mail or sending packages, post offices offer a place to meet neighbors and catch up on news, making them an influential realm of the public sphere. In Florida, sixteen new post offices were built between 1938 and 1946, and each was decorated with murals or relief sculptures paid for by the Treasury Department's Section of Painting and Sculpture. Florida's post office murals and sculptures, by fourteen different artists, include scenes of daily life, industry, the landscape, and history, and collectively, these scenes capture the dynamism of life and labor during the 1930s and 1940s.

Public parks and post offices are also spaces of controversy. The mission of the Florida Parks Service is "to provide resource-based recreation while preserving, interpreting, and restoring natural and cultural resources," but since its founding in 1935, the state agency has struggled to balance the needs of conservation and preservation with those of recreation. In the 1950s, Governor Lawton Chiles proposed building a prison in Tate's Hell State Forest, and in 2011 Governor Rick Scott tried to sell $50 million worth of park land to create golf courses. (According to the National Golf Association, Florida has more than one thousand golf courses, more than any other state.) Neither plan was successful, as citizens banded together to remind legislators that the beaches, swamps, oak hammocks, and dry prairies protected by Florida's state parks are not commodities awaiting human improvement. Instead, they are a key part of life in the Sunshine State. In fact, the Florida Park Service has expanded to one of the largest and most heavily used systems in the country. With 175 parks, 10 state trails, nearly 800,000 acres of protected land, and more than 27 million visitors annually, the Florida Park Service preserves and protects the state's scenic resources while generating $2.1 billion in revenue. For the department's efforts, it has been awarded the National Recreation and Parks Association gold medal for excellence three times, more than any other state in the country. At the same time, Florida has lost more wetlands than any other state; all of the state's mahogany has been harvested, as has much of its longleaf pine; and over one hundred species of wildlife have been pushed to the edge of extinction. Saltwater intrusion threatens the aquifer, and algae blooms and red tide kill thousands of fish and birds every year.

Florida's post office murals do not garner the same level of national attention as state parks or climate change, but they are important to their local communities and share an intimate connection to the landscape. In their very physicality, whether in the pigments, oils, and minerals extracted from the earth to make the paint; in the wood, metal, and horsehair used to make the brushes; or in the linen, cotton, and hemp used to create the canvases that were then adhered to the walls with a variety of types of glue, the material origins of post office murals reveal the ecologies of their making. Offering insights into an area's history, these paintings depict local industries, heroes, and topographies. Florida's murals engage with the importance of education to the establishment of DeFuniak Springs; logging and timber to the economies of Milton, Perry, and Jasper; and cotton to Madison. The natural landscape is both exploited and celebrated by muralists, as are the Indigenous and colonial histories their murals portray. For many early settlers of Florida, the area's wild nature, its swamps and forests, were overwhelming and threatening, and just as the Civilian Conservation Corps tamed the landscape by paving roads, blazing trails, building shelters, killing rattlesnakes and alligators, and planting azaleas, the Section's muralists domesticated the land by painting scenes of tractable land ready for development.

Today, some of these histories have come under scrutiny. Landscapes once viewed as a celebration of a town's industry, such as George Snow Hill's 1940 mural *Long Staple Cotton*, have been covered, and others have been moved, removed, destroyed, or lost. For now, many of these murals are still on display, and I hope you will make the time to see them before the chance is lost.

BIBLIOGRAPHY

Adams, Katherine, and Michael Keene. *Women, Art and the New Deal*. Jefferson, NC: McFarland, 2016.

Agee, William C. *The 1930s: Painting and Sculpture in America*. New York: Whitney Museum of American Art, 1968.

Arabindan-Kesson, Anna. *Black Bodies, White Gold: Art, Cotton, and Commerce in the Atlantic World*. Durham, NC: Duke University Press, 2021.

Baigell, Matthew. *The American Scene: American Painting of the 1930s*. New York, Praeger, 1974.

Beckert, Sven. *Empire of Cotton: A Global History*. New York: Alfred A. Knopf, 2014.

Beckford, George L. *Persistent Poverty: Underdevelopment in Plantation Economies of the Third World*. Barbados: University of the West Indies Press, 1999.

Beckham, Sue Bridwell. *Depression Post Office Murals and Southern Culture: A Gentle Reconstruction*. Baton Rouge: Louisiana State University Press, 1989.

Biddle, George. *An American Artist's Story*. Boston: Little, Brown and Co., 1939.

Blackmore, Lisa, and Liliana Gómez, eds. *Liquid Ecologies in Latin American and Caribbean Art*. London: Routledge, 2020.

Braddock, Alan C., and Christoph Irmscher, eds. *A Keener Perception: Ecocritical Studies in American Art History*. Tuscaloosa: University of Alabama Press, 2009.

Brinton, Daniel G. *A Guide-Book of Florida and the South, for Tourists, Invalids and Emigrants*. Lancaster: Wylie & Griest Press, 1869.

Brown, Milton W. *American Painting from the Armory Show to the Depression*. Princeton, NJ: Princeton University Press, 1955.

Bruce, Edward. *Art in Federal Buildings: An Illustrated Record of the Treasury Department's New Program in Painting and Sculpture*. Washington, D.C.: Art in Federal Buildings, 1936.

Bustard, Bruce I. *A New Deal for the Arts*. Washington, D.C.: National Archives and Records Administration, 1997.

Caldwell, Erskine, and Margaret Bourke-White. *You Have Seen Their Faces*. New York: Viking Press, 1937.

Carlisle, John C., and Darryl Jones. *A Simple and Vital Design: The Story of the Indiana Post Office Murals*. Indianapolis: Indiana Historical Society, 1995.

Contreras, Belisario R. *Tradition and Innovation in New Deal Art*. Lewisburg, PA: Bucknell University Press, 1983.

Coughlin, Maura, and Emily Gephart, eds. *Ecocriticism and the Anthropocene in Nineteenth-Century Art and Visual Culture*. New York: Routledge, 2019.

David, Jack E., and Raymond Arsenault, eds. *Paradise Lost? The Environmental History of Florida*. Gainesville: University Press of Florida, 2005.

Davis, Anita Price. *New Deal Art in North Carolina: The Murals, Sculptures, Reliefs, Paintings, Oils and Frescoes and Their Creators*. Jefferson, NC: McFarland, 2009.

Davis, Heather, and Etienne Turpin, eds. *Art in the Anthropocene: Encounters Among Aesthetics, Politics, Environments and Epistemologies.* Open Humanities Press, 2014. http://www.openhumanitiespress.org.

Demos, T.J. "Ecology-as-Intrasectionality." *Panorama: Journal of the Association of Historians of American Art* 5, no. 1 (Spring 2019). https://doi.org/10.24926/24716839.1699.

Demos, T.J., Emily Eliza Scott and Subhankar Banerjee. *The Routledge Companion to Contemporary Art, Visual Culture, and Climate Change.* London: Routledge, 2021.

DeVille, Taylor, and Craig Clary. "Post Office Mural Depicting Slavery Is Covered." *Washington Post*, October 17. 2020. www.washingtonpost.com.

Dorson, Richard M. *America in Legend.* New York: Pantheon Books, 1973.

Doss, Erika. "Looking at Labor: Images of Work in 1930s American Art." *Journal of Decorative and Propaganda Arts* 24 (2002): 230–57.

Fahlman, Betsy. *New Deal Art in Arizona.* Tucson: University of Arizona Press, 2009.

Falk, Peter Hastings, ed. *Who Was Who In American Art. 1564–1975: 400 Years of Artists in America.* Madison, CT: Sound View Press, 1985.

Freeman, Susan Hale. "Monument to Three Artists." *Update* 14, no. 3 (1987): 3–5.

Gibson, Jon, and Philip J. Carr, eds. *Signs of Power: The Rise of Cultural Complexity in the Southeast.* Tuscaloosa: University of Alabama Press, 2004.

Grunwald, Michael. *The Swamp: The Everglades, Florida, and the Politics of Paradise.* New York: Simon and Schuster, 2006.

Harris, Jonathan. *Federal Art and National Culture: The Politics of Identity in New Deal America.* New York: Cambridge University Press, 1995.

Henderson, Clay. *Forces of Nature: A History of Florida Land Conservation.* Gainesville: University Press of Florida, 2022.

Hoelscher, Steven. "Making Place, Making Race: Performances of Whiteness in the Jim Crow South." *Annals of the Association of American Geographers* 93, no. 3 (2003): 657–86.

Horton, Jessica. "Indigenous Artists against the Anthropocene." *Art Journal* 76, no. 2 (2017): 48–69.

Hull, Howard. *Tennessee Post Office Murals.* Johnson City, TN: Overmountain Press, 1996.

Jones, Alfred Haworth. "The Search for a Usable American Past in the New Deal Era." *American Quarterly* 23 (December 1971): 710–24.

Kalish, Evan. "USPS Officials Order Historic Murals Covered in 12 States; Considering Removal." *Postlandia,* September 1, 2020. https://blog.evankalish.com.

Kennedy, Roger G., and Ann Prentice Wagner. *1934: A New Deal for Artists.* Washington, D.C.: Smithsonian American Art Museum, 2009.

Kennedy, Roger G., and David Larkin. *When Art Worked: The New Deal, Art, and Democracy.* New York: Rizzoli, 2009.

Kersey, Harris, Jr. "The Florida Seminoles in the Depression and New Deal, 1933–1942: An Indian Perspective." *Florida Historical Quarterly* 65 (October 1986): 175–95.

Kleinberg, Eliot. *Palm Beach Past: The Best of "Post Time."* Charleston, SC: The History Press, 2006.

Kramer, Hilton. "Art: Projects of W.P.A. Revisited." *New York Times,* November 18, 1977.

Kroiz, Lauren. *Cultivating Citizens: The Regional Work of Art in the New Deal Era.* Berkeley: University of California Press, 2018.

Kusserow, Karl, and Alan C. Braddock, eds. *Nature's Nation: American Art and Environment*. Princeton, NJ: Princeton University Art Museum, 2018.

Lamonaca, Marianne. "Whose History Is It Anyway? New Deal Post Office Murals in South Florida." In *The New Deal in South Florida: Design, Policy, and Community Building, 1933–1940*, edited by John A. Stuart and John F. Stark Jr., 120–57. Gainesville: University Press of Florida, 2008.

Landrum, Ney C. *A Legacy of Green*. Tallahassee: Florida State Parks Association, 2013.

Linden, Diana. *Ben Shahn's New Deal Murals: Jewish Identity in the American Scene*. Detroit, MI: Wayne State University Press. 2015.

Living New Deal. Department of Geography, University of California, Berkeley. https://livingnewdeal.org.

Lyons, Maura. "An Embodied Landscape: Wounded Trees at Gettysburg." *American Art* 26, no. 3 (2012): 44–65.

Mack, Angela D., and Stephen G. Hoffius, eds. *Landscape of Slavery: The Plantation in American Art*. Columbia: University of South Carolina Press, 2007.

Maher, Neil M. *Nature's New Deal: The Civilian Conservation Corps and the Roots of the American Environmental Movement*. Oxford: Oxford University Press, 2009.

Mahoney, Eleanor. "Post Office Murals and Art for Federal Buildings: The Treasury Section of Painting and Sculpture in Washington State, 1934–1943." *The Great Depression in Washington State Project*. http://depts. washington.edu/depress/Section.shtml.

Maresca, Joseph. *WPA Buildings: Architecture and Art of the New Deal*. New York: Schiffer, 2017.

Marling, Karal Ann. *Wall-to-Wall America: A Cultural History of Post-Office Murals in the Great Depression*. Minneapolis: University of Minnesota Press, 1982.

Matthews, Eugene. "The Story of Starke." *Bradford County Telegraph*, Starke Centennial Issue, May 3, 1957.

McDonald, William F. *Federal Relief Administration and the Arts*. Columbus: Ohio State University Press, 1969.

McKinzie, Richard D. *The New Deal for Artists*. Princeton, NJ: Princeton University Press, 1972.

McKittrick, Katherine, and Clyde Woods. *Black Geographies and the Politics of Place*. Cambridge, MA: South End Press, 2007.

Mecklenburg, Virginia. *The Public as Patron: A History of the Treasury Department Mural Program*. College Park: University of Maryland Department of Art, 1979.

Melosh, Barbara. *Engendering Culture: Manhood and Womanhood in New Deal Public Art and Theater*. Washington, D.C.: Smithsonian Institution Press, 1991.

Monani, Salma, and Joni Adamson, eds. *Ecocriticism and Indigenous Studies: Conversations from Earth to Cosmos*. London: Routledge, 2016.

Musher, Sharon. *Democratic Art: The New Deal's Influence on American Culture*. Chicago: University of Chicago Press, 2015.

National Research Council. *Science and the Greater Everglades Ecosystem Restoration: An Assessment of the Critical Ecosystem Studies Initiative*. Washington, D.C.: National Academy Press, 2003.

Nelson, David. "When Modern Tourism Was Born: Florida at the World Fairs and on the World Stage in the 1930s." *Florida Historical Quarterly* 88, no. 4 (2010): 435–68.

Nelson, David J. *How the New Deal Built Florida Tourism: The Civilian Conservation Corps and State Parks*. Gainesville: University of Florida Press, 2019.

———. "Rejecting Paradise: Tourism, Conservation, and the Birth of the Modern Florida Cracker in the 1930s." *Florida Historical Quarterly* 96, no. 3 (2018): 328 71.

O'Connor, Francis V., ed. *Art for the Millions: Essays from the 1930s by Artists and Administrators of the WPA Federal Art Project.* Greenwich, CT: New York Graphic Society, 1973.

———. *Federal Support for the Visual Arts: The New Deal and Now.* Greenwich, CT: New York Graphic Society, 1969.

Parisi, Philip. *The Texas Post Office Murals: Art for the People.* College Station: Texas A&M University Press, 2004.

Park, Marlene, and Gerald E. Markowitz. *Democratic Vistas: Post Offices and Public Art in the New Deal.* Philadelphia: Temple University Press, 1984.

Pierce, Charles W. *Pioneer Life in Southeast Florida.* Coral Cables: University of Miami Press, 1970.

Pittman, Craig. "Battling Florida's Government to Protect Public Lands." *Sarasota Magazine,* March 2014. www.sarasotamagazine.com.

———. "Controversial Public Service Commission Member Will Be Next Boss of Florida's Parks." *Tampa Bay Times,* December 21, 2016. www.tampabay.com.

Pratt, Theodore. *The Barefoot Mailman.* New York: Hawthorn Books, 1943.

Rankin, T.J. "Grayling Post Office Houses a Unique Piece of American Art History." *Crawford County Avalanche,* February 14, 2013. www.crawfordcountyavalanche.com.

Raynor, Patricia. "Off the Wall: New Deal Post Office Murals." *EnRoute* 6, no. 4 (1997). www.postalmuseum.si.edu.

Robinson, Jim, and Mark Andrews. *Flashbacks: The Story of Central Florida's Past.* Orlando, FL: Orange County Historical Society, 1995.

Rowin, Fran. "Federally Sponsored Murals in Florida Post Offices During the Depression." Master's thesis, University of Miami, 1976.

Schwan, Gary. "Barefoot Mailman Art Gets First Class Handing." *Palm Beach Post*, August 18, 1984.

Shofner, Jerrell. "Roosevelt's 'Tree Army': The Civilian Conservation Corps in Florida." *Florida Historical Quarterly* 65 (April 1987): 433–56.

Siboroski, Paul Michael. "Reflections of the Community: Post Office Murals in Florida Commissioned Under the New Deal." Master's thesis, University of Florida, 1990.

Slipp, Naomi. "Gilded Age Dining: Eco-Anxiety, Fisheries Management and the Presidential China of Rutherford B. Hayes." In *Ecocriticism and the Anthropocene in Nineteenth-Century Art and Visual Culture*, edited by Maura Coughlin and Emily Gephart, 135–44. New York: Routledge, 2019.

Slovic, Scott, Swarnalatha Rangarajan and Vidya Sarveswaran. *Routledge Handbook of Ecocriticism and Environmental Communication*. London: Routledge, 2019.

Starr, Sandra. "Find New Deal-Era Murals in the Old Tallahassee Post Office Building, Indians! In the Post Office," *Tallahassee Magazine*, January–February 2014.

Taylor, Nick. *American-Made: The Enduring Legacy of the WPA: When FDR Put the Nation to Work*. New York: Bantam Books, 2009.

Upton, Dell. *What Can and Can't Be Said: Race, Uplift, and Monument Building in the Contemporary South*. New Haven, CT: Yale University Press, 2015.

Vlach, John Michael. *The Planter's Prospect: Privilege and Slavery in Plantation Paintings*. Chapel Hill: University of North Carolina Press, 2002.

Watson, Forbes. "Chance in a Thousand: Treasury Department's Section of Painting and Sculpture Competitions." *American Magazine of Art*, August 1935.

Watson, Keri. *In the Eyes of the Hungry: Florida's Changing Landscape*. Orlando: University of Central Florida Art Gallery, 2017.

Way, Albert G. *Conserving Southern Longleaf: Herbert Stoddard and the Rise of Ecological Land Management*. Athens: University of Georgia Press, 2011.

Widmer, Randolph J. *The Evolution of the Calusa: A Nonagricultural Chiefdom on the Southwest Florida Coast*. Tuscaloosa: University of Alabama Press, 1988.

The WPA Guide to Florida: The Federal Writers' Project Guide to 1930s Florida. New York: Pantheon Books, 1939.

ABOUT THE AUTHOR

Keri Watson (PhD, Florida State University, 2010) is an associate professor of art history at the University of Central Florida, a co-executive editor for *Panorama: Journal of the Association of Historians of American Art* and a speaker for the Florida Humanities Council. She is the coauthor, with Julia Listengarten, of *Visual and Performing Arts Collaborations in Higher Education: Transdisciplinary Practices* (Palgrave Macmillan, 2023); the coauthor, with Keidra Daniels Navaroli, of *This Is America: Reviewing the Art of the United States* (Oxford University Press, 2023); and coeditor, with Timothy W. Hiles, of *The Routledge Companion to Art and Disability* (2022). Her research has been published in journals and edited collections including *Southern Cultures*, the *Journal of Surrealism and the Americas*, *Mosaic: A Journal for the Interdisciplinary Study of Literature*, *Museums and Social Issues: A Journal of Reflective Discourse*, the *Journal of Literary & Cultural Disability Studies*, the *Eudora Welty Review*, and the *Journal of Museum Education*, among others, and it has been recognized and supported by a Fulbright Fellowship and grants from the National Endowment for the Arts, Arts Midwest, the Terra Foundation for American Art, the Institute of Museum and Library Services, the Florida Humanities Council, and the Society for the Preservation of American Modernists. She lives in Oviedo, Florida, with her family.